Jan Timman pays tribute to the Fifth World Champion

NEW!

T0001574

World Champion Max Euwe, who held the title from 1935-1937, is one of the greatest chess players in history. *Max Euwe's Best Games* is the first outstanding collection of games of this 'efficient, man-eating tiger', as the American grandmaster Reuben Fine once called Euwe. The book offers eighty of Euwe's games annotated with great clarity by Jan Timman, who knew Euwe very well. Timman made many discoveries in Euwe's best and most famous games but has also unearthed several lesser-known brilliancies.

NEW IN CHESS

ENJOY THE BEST GAME. EVER.

14

62

105

'Sometimes I would say quite strange things. Just like ChatGPT sometimes creates the perfect answer, very careful and very accurate, and sometimes you don't know what it's saying'

(Ding Liren, page 39)

'Chess is always exciting if you look for nuances.'

After five hours of play, Bobby lifted his rook and said...

CONTRIBUTORS TO THIS ISSUE
James Altucher, Erwin l'Ami, Fabiano Caruana, Vladimir Fedoseev, Jorden van Foreest, Anish Giri, Dommaraju Gukesh, John Henderson, Justin Horton, Maxim Notkin, Margeir Petursson, Judit Polgar, Joseph G. Ponterotto, Matthew Sadler, Chad Smith, Peter Svidler, Jan Timman, Thomas Willemze
PHOTOS AND ILLUSTRATIONS
Stev Bonhage, David Llada, Lennart Ootes, Omar Oskarsson, Berend Vonk
COVER DESIGN Hélène Bergmans

The Royal Game

I f you wander the streets of the historical centre of The Hague, there is a fair chance that you will be challenged to a game of chess. Every Saturday members of chess club 'En Passant' take to the streets and set up their tables at varying locations in the 'International City of Justice'.

They first did so during the pandemic, when their club had to close its doors. Independent of the weather they played their games outdoors, often braving the elements wearing hats and winter coats. Or basking in the sunshine on summer days.

When the pandemic ended, the club reopened, but the attraction of playing chess in the open air proved too strong to abandon their outings. One of their favourite spots is the square opposite Noordeinde Palace in the Court Quarter. Noordeinde Palace is the official workplace of the Dutch King Willem-Alexander and Queen Maxima. Certainly a fitting place for the royal game. ∎

Lighting chess

How many times have you made a bad move due to poor lighting conditions in the tournament hall? But not anymore, for here comes the latest must-have gizmo, the Masteek Light-Up Chess wireless LED set, which the company's advertising claims with its unique lighting system, will only add 'an extra level of excitement and drama to the game'.

It features a unique design with pieces that light up wirelessly using electromagnetic induction. The board itself is white, and when the pieces are placed perpendicularly above it, they light up. The white squares also light up with the pieces, creating an amazing visual effect.

The set doesn't require batteries in the pieces, as the board powers everything. The board is equipped with wireless induction electronics that

That's what we call lighting chess!

transfer the energy and powers-up the very artistic and futuristic pieces. Each piece is installed with an LED that lights up the glass core.

You can check out the Kickstarter campaign to get your own Masteek Light-Up Chess set.

The wild cat of chess

There was a time when PUMA was the brand of choice for footballing legends Pele, Maradona, George Best, Johan Cruyff and Eusebio. Now the Wild Cat has gone

from the beautiful game to the royal game!

PUMA and brand ambassador Magnus Carlsen have teamed up to launch an iconic sneaker as a tribute to the game of chess. The collaboration features a new design based on

Magnus with his favourite sneaker.

PUMA's classic Clyde model – but with its very own chessic twist.

The new sneakers are made with a premium leather upper that features a chessboard-inspired texture, giving them a unique and sophisticated look. The shoe also includes a contrasted suede form strip, a heel overlay, and a quarter PUMA logo with Magnus Signature in foil print.

'It's an incredible honour to be part of the first chess-inspired sneaker that PUMA has ever made', says Carlsen. 'I'm glad that with the Clyde, we chose a style with a rich culture and basketball heritage. It shows off my personality, combining my love of chess with my passion for basketball.'

To further showcase their chess-inspired design, the sneakers come with a woven tongue label with PUMA branding and a chess figure. The shoes also feature chess figures as lace jewels in black and white colours. Additionally, the synthetic leather sock liner boasts a chess-themed design, with the king piece showcased on the right shoe and the queen piece on the left shoe.

Centennial chess

We hear so much about prepubescent prodigies in chess these days, so we were more than overjoyed to hear news about one of the 'old in chess' brigade: US World War II veteran Lou Giarrusso celebrated his 100th birthday in style by rolling up to play in a chess tournament in East Greenwich, Rhode Island.

Lou started playing competitively in 1963 and serves as an inspiration to all of us-old and young. On his landmark birthday, on May 11, the very sprightly centenarian played in the Once-in-a-Lifetime Inaugural Championship Cup Event held at the New England Institute of Technology, where he was presented with a chessboard birthday cake, plaques and certificates, and a trophy for his lifetime achievements in the game.

And just two days later, the local Ocean State Chess Association launched the 'Louis Giarrusso Centennial Cup' also at NE Tech, where beloved tournament regular Lou also played! 'I don't think anyone has played at this age in registered

Lou Giarrusso (100) still has the moves.

tournaments', said event organiser Frank DelBonis to the local media. 'How often do you see something like this – playing competitive chess at 100?'

It occurs a little more often than you would think, because Lou now joins a very select club of two alongside Spaniard Manuel Alvarez Escudero (b.1921), with both centenarians having played in tournaments held to commemorate their 100th birthday!

Rebel with a chess set

In Hollywood mythology, James Dean is hard to beat. He had made only three films – *East of Eden*, *Rebel Without a Cause* and *Giant* – when he died way, way too young in a car crash aged just 24 in 1955. Any Dean memorabilia is eagerly sought after, and we took an interest in a recent auction as it promised many previously unseen small items showing a new side to the star.

A cache of nearly 400 personal items was listed via Nate D Sanders Auctions that came from the estate of Dean's agent, Jane Deacy. The lot included many personal letters, ballpoint pens, his motorbike registration documents, a signed iconic silver gelatin photo from a 1955 motorbike session, and his Warner Bros contract signed by Dean for East of Eden, which was expected to fetch thousands of dollars.

Dean was also a keen chess player, which was the reason this auction

James Dean with his favourite pocket chess set.

piqued our interest. But alas, apparently no one has yet discovered what happened to his favourite vintage Drueke pocket chess set that he always carried with him. Dean was

famously photographed in deep thought over it for a studio PR shot, while a canary sat on his shoulder seemingly as if kibitzing moves into the Tinseltown star's ear.

Daily Fail

Not for nothing in the UK is the Daily Mail more politely nicknamed the 'Daily Fail'. And the scaremongering right-wing tabloid more

> **Chinese man wins the World Chess Championship for the first time in the tournament's history after decades of US and Russian dominance**
>
> By Daily Mail Reporter
> 20:12 EDT 30 Apr 2023 , updated 20:25 EDT 30 Apr 2023

than lived up to its reputation for failing even to make the most basic of fact checks when it came to its online story of Ding Liren becoming the 17th World Champion.

The unnamed 'Daily Mail Reporter' lazily led with the strapline 'Chinese man wins the World Chess Championship for the first time in the tournament's history after decades of US and Russian dominance.'

There were many who were quick to point out to Lord Rothermere's rag that a certain Norwegian might well have something to say on that bold call with his dominance over the past decade, not to mention his Indian predecessor, a six-time ex-world champion!

Pole-axed in Poland

As the $1.4m 2023 Grand Chess Tour circus moved from Bucharest to Warsaw for the Superbet Rapid and Blitz Poland, all eyes were on the wildcard invite for the now ex-world champion Magnus Carlsen. But things didn't exactly go to script for the world No 1, who still has the two

rapid and blitz crowns to his name and was the hot favourite to win.

Sans the main crown, a free-spirited Carlsen attempted to be a crowd-pleaser in his opening round encounter against Radoslaw Wojtaszek by playing the Polish Defence (1.d4 b5) against the Pole, who duly pole-axed the ex-world champion, much to the delight of the very patriotic Polish crowds! After the debacle, Wojtaszek, Poland's No 2, said: 'When he chose 1...b5, I thought let's play, let's make some normal moves. My approach was to play active chess, and that's what I thought gave me victory.'

Carlsen, who joins Boris Spassky in the exclusive club of being the only two world champions to play the Polish Defence, was in trouble by move nine before resigning at move 38. After the game he commented: 'I haven't played or studied much chess recently, so it was showing,' before he went on to draw his next five games that started rumours swirling that he was set to 'call time on his career'.

Radoslaw Wojtaszek
Magnus Carlsen
Warsaw Superbet Rapid 2023 (1.2)
1.d4 b5 There it is!
2.e4 ♗b7 3.♗d3 ♘f6 4.♘d2 c5 5.c3 cxd4 6.cxd4 e6 7.♘gf3 ♘c6 8.0-0 a6 9.♖e1 ♗e7 10.d5!

Finely timed, as this leaves the black king stranded in the middle of the board. **10...exd5 11.e5 ♘h5 12.♘b3 g6 13.♗h6 ♖g8 14.♗e3 ♘g7 15.♘c5 ♕c7?!** Better was

In his first-round game against Radoslaw Wojtaszek, Magnus Carlsen found out that playing the Polish Defence is more likely to lead to hair-raising problems than to pole position.

15...♗xc5 16.♗xc5 ♘e6 17.♗d6 h5 and looking to hold this position. **16.♖c1 ♘e6 17.♘xb7 ♕xb7 18.♗f1 ♗b4 19.♖e2 ♘e7 20.♖ec2 ♘f5 21.♗g5 ♗e7 22.♗f6 ♘fg7 23.♕d3 ♗xf6 24.exf6 ♘h5 25.♕c3! ♖d8**

26.a3?! The killer move was 26.♕e5, leaving Black's position a wreck. **26...♕b8 27.g3 g5 28.♖e1!** Threatening ♕c5! **28...g4 29.♘d4 ♖g5 30.♗d3 ♖e5 31.♘f5?!** After 31.♖ce2! Black is in dire straits. **31...♖xe1+?** In time trouble, Carlsen missed that 31...d4! seeming-

ly holds. **32.♕xe1 ♘xf6 33.♕b4!**

Further compromising Black's hopeless position. **33...d6 34.♕c3 ♘d7 35.♕h8+ ♘df8 36.♕f6**

36...♘g6 If 36...♕b7 37.a4! and White is either capturing twice on b5 or playing ♗xa6! mating. **37.♖e2 ♕c7 38.♘g7+** Black resigned.

Despite the jittery start of one loss and six games without a win, Carlsen staged a recovery of sorts on the final day of the rapid, with a much-needed brace of wins (with wins counting double) over Romanian back-markers Bogdan-Daniel Deac and Kirill Shevchenko. Placed mid-table heading into the blitz, it was going to be a big ask even for the Norwegian to overhaul the pace set by popular front-runner Jan-Krzysztof Duda on his home soil.

But Carlsen defied all the talk of his imminent retirement by winning seven games in a row to finish on 24/36 to capture the top prize of $40,000 plus 13 GCT points. The Norwegian was chased all the way to the final round by Duda, but held his nerve and a draw in a thrilling 124-move marathon against the Polish No.1.

Here's a small sample of Carlsen's sharpness when he was on the rampage.

Magnus Carlsen
Wesley So
Warsaw Superbet Blitz 2023 (11.4)

position after 53...b3

A difficult position to convert given that this is blitz, but Carlsen found a very efficient way to continue his winning streak for a seventh straight win with **54.♕b5+ ♔a3 55.♕xb3+!! ♘xb3 56.♘c2+**

Carlsen joins Boris Spassky in the exclusive club of the only two world champions to play the Polish Defence

Black resigned.

Duda finished second with $30,000 and 10 GCT points, while Wesley So and Maxime Vachier-Lagrave tied for third and fourth places to pocket $22,500 and 7.5 GCT points each.

With a wry smile etched on his face at the final presser, Carlsen was quick to quip about his comeback victory: 'Nice to show that my retirement only lasted a couple of days!'

Death of a wordsmith

It was with sadness we learned of the recent death of Martin Amis, the gifted bad-boy novelist acclaimed for capturing the zeitgeist of the 1980s and 1990s. With a body of work spanning 50 years, he leaves 15 novels, two short-story collections, one memoir and seven book-length works of history and journalism – which, lest we not forget, also contained some very profound insights on chess, the chess world, and the players who play the game.

With the glitzy literary chicanery that became Amis' trademark, he wrote about the epic Kasparov v Karpov matches of the mid-to-late 1980s in *Visiting Mrs Nabokov And Other Excursions*, and then the Kasparov v Short match in 1993 on his home turf of London for several leading broadsheets and periodicals, which was subsequently reproduced in his book *The War against Cliché. Essays and Reviews, 1971-2000*. The author states, in his own inimitable style, that it is the complexity of chess that gives it its beauty, and warns that

diminishing the difficulty could rob the game of its mystique.

'Chess waits in the wings, taking deep breaths, ready to burst on the stage as a planetary spectator sport... Chess offers its audience the soap opera of opposed personalities in genuinely bitter combat, deploying

Martin Amis: profound insights on chess and the chess world.

an unbounded repertoire of feint, bluff, trap, poeticism, profundity, brilliancy, together with a complementary array of blunders, howlers, squanderings... What stands in its way? Not the epic slowness of the game, or its frieze-like immobility. What stands in the way is the gap, the chasm, the abyss that lies between the watcher and the watched...'

And with those profound observations, we can also reveal that our editor once tentatively reached out to Amis with a view to writing a column for NIC. Not even expecting a reply, one promptly came, with the notorious literary *enfant terrible*

very courteously and politely saying that that he had to turn down the offer, being 'too busy to take on such a commitment'.

All played out?

In the May issue of BBC Science Focus Magazine, reader Lucy Metcalfe, from Liverpool, was looking for an answer to her chess-related question in their 'fascinating new Q&As every month' feature. She asks: 'In the past 500 years of modern chess, have we even come close to playing all iterations of the game?'

We're sure a simple 'yes' or a 'no' would have sufficed, but with this being a science journal of some repute, it was tasked to Oxford physicist Robert Matthews to come up with a more exacting answer: 'The modern game of chess is around 500 years old, so to put a rough upper limit on the total number of games played so far, let's assume around one per cent of people who have lived since then have played a different game of chess every day for 50 years. That means that around 10 million million games of chess have been played...'

Confused already? Yes, so were we; but the professor continued to blow our minds by further adding: 'That sounds a lot but each move in chess opens up around 38 legal new moves, and a typical chess match consists of around 40 or so moves per player. So the total number of moves possible is around 38 to the power 80, which works out at a staggering 10 to the power 126 – far larger than the number of particles in the visible Universe. So no, we're not even close to exhausting the possibilities of chess.'

So good to know then! ∎

'Over the past 500 years, 10 million million games of chess have been played, but we are not even close to exhausting the possiblities'

Different game

I am reacting to a letter from CM Markus Müller published in NIC 2023/3. He was critical of Chess960, also known as Fischer Random Chess. He is right in some aspects, as there are indeed few Chess960 tournaments. Mr Müller writes that '*knowing endgames by heart is regarded as a sign of true mastery but apparently this does not apply to the very beginning of the game*'. It is a clever observation, although I would like to add that it is just one sign of true mastery, along with the knowledge of typical plans, precise calculation and good intuition. It is nice to know many ♖+♙ vs. ♖ endgames by heart, but without the other skills a player might easily fail to reach them.

The statement about Magnus Carlsen being 'tired of our venerable ordinary chess' looks exaggerated. Top players usually need much longer opening preparation than other players, and this is especially true for the world championship matches. Studying openings might be interesting, but doing so several hours per day is less attractive.

I am certainly not fed-up with standard chess. I am playing a lot and preparing a lot, but it is tiring, as there is more opening theory than ever before. (In a way the previous generations played a different game.)

This is also one of the reasons why I love playing Chess960 so much. In standard chess, the game might sometimes steer into a quick draw, particularly if you are playing with Black and your opponent does not want to take big risks. When the players prepare for a game for three hours, they might lack the energy at the board and consequently either play more peacefully, or make more mistakes in complicated positions.

When reading about fed-up individuals, I am wondering if Mr Müller also means Bobby Fischer. The retired champion also heavily promoted the electronic clock and play with increment. The electronic clock was commonly called 'Fischer clock' at the beginning on this century and it has eventually prevailed. I do not expect Chess960 to prevail in the foreseeable future, but it has every right to live alongside with standard chess, which is what most proponents of Chess960 are hoping for. True, many players, including Mr Müller, do not want to play Chess960 for various legitimate reasons, but no one forces them to leave standard chess. (Such an effort would be hopeless anyway.)

While there are indeed very few Chess960 tournaments, there are many players willing to participate in more Chess960 events, but very few sponsors and organizers. Many famous grandmasters happily play Chess960 when having a good opportunity. I could name Magnus Carlsen,

Letter of the Month

Not quite the same

In his article "Ducking a fight" in New In Chess 2023/3, Jan Timman expressed disagreement with equating Carlsen's refusal to defend his title to the situation that aroused after Alekhine's death. This made for an interesting article, and for a nice excuse to revisit two thrilling games. Yet, a couple of his statements made me have similar feelings. First, it is said that only Smyslov had previously managed Nepomniachtchi's achievement of winning two consecutive Candidates tournaments. While strictly correct, it is also true that Boris Spassky, Viktor Korchnoi and Anatoly Karpov also won two back-to-back Candidates cycles, albeit in match and not in tournament format.

In all the ensuing matches, the champion was there to defend his title and, therefore, the Challengers got the opportunity to avenge a previous defeat, something that Spassky managed to do. A pity, indeed, for Nepo and chess that this time it was different. Then, Jan argues that "only twice in the history of chess" has a world champion refused to play against a Challenger, referring to Alekhine skipping for many years a fight against Capablanca and Kramnik avoiding a rematch against Kasparov. This comparison looks a bit forced to me, for one reason. While Alekhine and Kramnik avoided a dangerous opponent, thus increasing their chances to remain champions, Carlsen refused to play at the cost of losing the world championship. This looks closer to what Bobby Fischer did in 1975. Not ideal, but not quite the same form the point of view of sportsmanship.

Fernando Luis
Zaragoza, Spain

Wesley So, Hikaru Nakamura, Levon Aronian, Peter Svidler, Vladimir Fedoseev, Gata Kamsky and many others. Whenever there are Chess960 tournaments with a nice prize fund, many strong players participate. I have played 15 over-the-board Chess960 tournaments, but only one since 2018, as there have been very few opportunities. It is great that there are some online Chess960 events, but online chess is not everyone's cup of tea and has its own problems.

The openings in Chess960 might be described as strange, unusual or fresh, depending on your attitude to the game. There desire to play something fresh rather than 20 theoretical moves or dubious sidelines is completely legitimate. And the middlegames and especially endgames in Chess960 usually look very standard. Most of the Chess960 supporters are just willing to see significantly more tournaments. Such an objective should not threaten standard chess in any way.

David Navara
Czech Republic

Bobby Fischer was right

My proposal for reforming chess is a radical shift to Fischer Random. It is time to acknowledge that in hindsight, Bobby Fischer was 100% right in his assessment that limitless opening preparation is stifling the creativity of the game of chess, certainly now that engines have become so dominant in opening preparations. Memorization and engine power are trumping skills and creativity. Unleashing our skills and creative forces from the very first move onwards is so much more fun and so much more challenging, both for amateurs and for professional players! Your excellent magazine 2022#8 of December 2022 shows clearly that even the world's top players, including Magnus Carlsen, enjoy playing Fischer Random more because of that exact reason. He speaks of its 'massive potential'. So the key question is then: what is holding us back? Why wouldn't New in Chess and indeed, the world's number 1 rated chess player with his powerful company Play Magnus Group, start promoting a radical shift towards making Fischer Random mainstream? By adopting this new mission, New in Chess and Magnus Carlsen would pay tribute to one of the greatest chess players, while helping to safeguard the future of our beautiful game.

Noé van Hulst
Paris, France

COLOPHON

PUBLISHER: Remmelt Otten
EDITOR-IN-CHIEF:
Dirk Jan ten Geuzendam
HONORARY EDITOR: Jan Timman
CONTRIBUTING EDITOR: Anish Giri
EDITORS: John Kuipers, René Olthof
PRODUCTION: Joop de Groot
TRANSLATOR: Piet Verhagen
SALES AND ADVERTISING: Edwin van Haastert
© No part of this magazine may be reproduced, stored in a retrieval system or transmitted in any form or by any means, recording or otherwise, without the prior permission of the publisher.

NEW IN CHESS
P.O. BOX 1093
1810 KB ALKMAAR
THE NETHERLANDS

PHONE: 00-31-(0)72-51 27 137
SUBSCRIPTIONS: nic@newinchess.com
EDITORS: editors@newinchess.com

WWW.NEWINCHESS.COM

Write and win!

If your letter to the editor gets selected as 'Letter of the Month', you will receive a book by Jan Timman signed by the author. Or you can opt for a free one-year extension of your subscription.

Write your letter to:
New In Chess, P.O. Box 1093
1810 KB Alkmaar, The Netherlands
e-mail: editors@newinchess.com
Letters may be edited or abridged

Caruana claims spoils in Bucharest

Never getting into any trouble, Fabiano Caruana edged out his rivals in the Superbet Classic to claim the $100,000 winner's check. Arriving straight from Astana, brand-new world champion Ding Liren lacked energy and motivation and had to take a back seat.

by DIRK JAN TEN GEUZENDAM

The eighth season of the Grand Chess Tour, the brainchild of former World Champion Garry Kasparov, kicked off with the Superbet Classic in Bucha-rest. The 2023 edition of the GCT consists of five tournaments, three of them rapid & blitz competitions. Just like this first leg in the capital of Romania, the final leg, the tradi-tional Sinquefield Cup in St. Louis coming November, will be a classical tournament.

The overall $1.4 million prize fund is provided by the two major sponsors of the GCT, the Superbet Foundation and the Saint Louis

The Superbet Classic very much was a classical tournament of the old style with lots of spectators and autograph hunters coming to the venue

American shows fine form as Grand Chess Tour kicks off

much was a classical tournament of the old style, with lots of spectators and autograph hunters coming to the venue, the Grand Hotel Bucharest, to watch their heroes in the flesh. Likewise, Romanian GMs like Liviu-Dieter Nisipeanu and Mihail Marin dropped by, and for most of the rounds the legendary Florin Gheorghiu (of beating Bobby Fischer at the Havana 1966 Olympiad fame) could be seen in the audience. As a special treat, Garry Kasparov was present for several rounds and was kind enough to make Ding Liren's first official move as World Champion.

No choice

The field in Bucharest promised excitement and intrigue, if only because it was hard to predict in what form and mood several of the grandmasters would arrive. The mysterious Alireza Firouzja played his first clas-

sical chess since his victory in the Sinquefield Cup last September (a win that, together with his win in the Saint Louis Rapid & Blitz, made him the overall winner of the 2022 Grand Chess Tour). Meanwhile, the Iranian-born Frenchman and his family have moved from the outskirts of Paris to a more central location in the French capital, and there has been much talk about his apparent wish to make a name for himself in fashion. How this will impact his chess is anyone's guess.

The presence of brand-new World Champion Ding Liren and the man he vanquished, Ian Nepomniachtchi, attracted even more press attention. While the organizers were clearly happy to welcome both world championship finalists straight from Astana, there were good grounds to wonder how much energy they would have left and

Chess Club, 'both non-profit organizations that support chess education and the mission to expand the game of chess to a worldwide audience'. The $350,000 prize fund of both classical events is double that of the rapid & blitz events, and first prize in Bucharest was $100,000.

With the global betting market growing at a worrying pace, it can hardly come as a surprise that betting companies have also entered chess as large-scale sponsors. After all, one of the biggest sponsors of the number one player in the world is a betting company. Still, it feels a bit awkward to see a game that should attract youngsters because of the skills it requires being financially supported by an industry that wants its clientele to believe in chance and good fortune.

Still, the Superbet Classic very

We don't know what he said , but Garry Kasparov had Ding Liren in stitches when he welcomed him at the start of his first official game as world champion.

how motivated they would be. Both indicated that they would rather have gone home, but as full tour members they were contractually obliged to play both classical legs (and two out of three rapid & blitz legs). Ding Liren understood that he had no real choice, but Nepomniachtchi repeated his request to withdraw after his Round 4 loss against Fabiano Caruana. In a position in which almost any move would have got a 0.00 verdict from the engines, he had managed to find the only move that allowed his opponent to play for a win. Days later, he still couldn't believe it and complained that after two hours his brain had just stopped working.

Ding and Nepo reached their nadir in Round 7, when they both lost their games and dramatically dropped to the two bottom places in the standings. It was a sad sight, and not something they had deserved after their spectacular match in Astana, which had captivated fans around the globe.

While Nepo went under against Firouzja, Ding Liren fell victim to the creativity and attacking skills of Anish Giri. With this win, the Dutchman accomplished a unique double feat. Following his win against Magnus Carlsen in Wijk aan Zee, he could now claim that he had defeated two reigning World Champions in classical chess in one year.

Anish Giri
Ding Liren
Bucharest GCT Superbet Chess Classic 2023 (7)
Italian Game, Giuoco Pianissimo

1.e4 e5 2.♘f3 ♘c6 3.♗c4
Curiously enough, Ding Liren had only faced the Spanish during the World Championship match in

Astana. I was eager to find out if he still recalled all the move orders of the Italian.
3...♘f6 4.d3 ♗c5 5.♗g5

Sometimes it's possible to pin the knight, but Black can often prevent this with ...h7-h6. But sometimes he can't.
5...h6 6.♗h4 d6
Another theme is to unpin the knight

'I was eager to find out if Ding still recalled all the move orders of the Italian'

with ...♗e7, but Ding stays true to his principles and goes for the more ambitious way to deal with the pin, an eventual ...g7-g5.
7.c3 a5 8.♘bd2 ♗a7 9.a4

An interesting cat and mouse game, with both sides delaying short castling. Ding is first to blink.
9...0-0
It would have been possible to continue delaying castling, but in that case,

Black would have had to play a more committal move. He could have played ...g5 first, but then the dangerous looking h2-h4 break might be on the cards.

10.h3! This was bad news for Ding, who was surely hoping that White would castle at some point. Now ...g5 looks dangerous, although it is not clear how Black should prepare for it, since ...♔h8 might backfire due to the g4! push.
10...g5? Principled, but the coming sacrifice is too dangerous in this particular version. Instead, Black could try to play it safer. As said, 10...♔h8?! wasn't great in view of 11.g4!, but 10...♗e6 wouldn't have been too bad.

11.♘xg5!
This sacrifice, although typical, is rarely very strong. Here it works really well, though, because White has already played the very useful move h3 and delayed castling short, which wouldn't necessarily combine well with a kingside attack.
11...hxg5 12.♗xg5 ♔g7
Black needs this move, since ♕f3 is coming anyway.

13.♕f3 An automatic move.
13...♗e6

The most sensible decision. Black's ideas here are mainly connected with ...♘c6-b8-d7, as far as I could understand. My preparation hadn't gone much deeper, and the only thing I recollected was that in a position very similar to this one, there was the idea of ...♗e6 ♘f1 ...♗xf2+ ♔e2!.

14.♘f1!

Ding Liren was the second reigning world champion to lose to Anish Giri in 2023, as the Dutchman had also beaten Magnus Carlsen in Wijk aan Zee.

14...♖h8

This clever move confused me a bit. 14...♗xf2+ looks very tempting, but the refutation is very elegant: 15.♔e2!, avoiding all ...♘xe4 tactics to unpin the knight. The f2-bishop is still hanging and the pressure on the f6-knight will soon become unbearable, as ♘h2 is coming and the f-file is now open.

14...♘b8 is what I had expected: 15.♘g3 ♘bd7 16.♘h5+ ♔g6 17.♗h4. This would probably force Black to give up the queen, with some material advantage for White.

15.♘e3!

This is the way to go. I discarded 15.♘g3 due to 15...♔g6 16.h4? ♗g4! 17.♗xf6 ♕d7!, and White's queen is trapped in rather thematic fashion.

15...♕e7

Black maintains the tension, which confused me even more. I kept calculating ...♘b8 on every move, as well as captures on e3 and c4. And here I castled queenside intuitively, having overlooked some concrete issues.

15...♗xc4 would have lost immediately to 16.♘g4!.

And 15...♗xe3 16.fxe3 ♘b8 doesn't work here either: 17.0-0 ♘bd7 18.♕g3!.

ANALYSIS DIAGRAM

I don't think I saw this (the point being the move that follows), but the computer is helping out, now that the game is over: 18...♘h5 19.♗xe6! (the complications will work in favour

of White) 19...♘xg3 (or 19...fxe6 20.♕g4) 20.♖xf7+ ♔g6 21.♗xd8 ♘c5 22.♖f3 ♘e2+ 23.♔h2 ♖axd8 24.♗c4, and White is winning.

16.0-0-0?

Sometimes you make a move and you feel it is bad. My idea was to meet ...♘b8 with d4, but I had underestimated the ♘f5+ idea, although it was what I had initially intended.

The better move order was 16.♖f1!. After 16...♘b8, 17.♘f5+ is deadly: 17...♗xf5 18.♕xf5 ♘bd7 (I obviously saw potential for White here, but I wasn't sure if Black would manage to drum up some counterplay with ...c6/...d5 or some ...♖ag8/...♔f8 ideas) 19.0-0-0 c6 20.♖de1 (it is important to take care of the e3-square before going f4, since ...♗e3+ is there) 20...b5 21.♗a2 b4 (his counterplay is not fast enough) 22.f4, and Black's position is collapsing under White's threats.

As he came out of the playing hall after his win against Ding Liren, Anish Giri was beleaguered by fans asking for autographs and selfies.

16...♖ag8?
Missing more or less the only chance to get back into the game. I think both of us were confused at this point, so we both resorted to making some random and vaguely useful moves. Here 16...♗e3+ actually works for Black: 17.fxe3 ♘b8! (not 17...♗xc4? because of 18.♖hf1!) 18.♖hf1 ♘bd7.

ANALYSIS DIAGRAM

A move ago this operation wasn't good enough for Black, but now, having castled long, White has lost a tempo compared to short castling, when the rook would appear on f1 immediately. White has to be accurate to maintain the balance: 19.♗d5! (if 19.♖f2 then 19...♗xc4 20.dxc4 ♕e6 21.♖df1 ♘h7! is better for Black, while after 19.♕g3, 19...♘h5! 20.♗f6+ ♔h7!, the move I had missed is also good for Black) 19...c6 Black has options at this point. 20.♕g3 ♔f8 (if 20...♘h5 then the weakness of the d6-pawn

will be crucial after 21.♗xe7, when White reaches an endgame) 21.♖xf6 (a forced sequence) 21...♘xf6 22.♕f3 ♘xd5 23.♗xe7+ ♘xe7 24.d4, with a very unclear position, which the engine evaluates as roughly balanced.
17.♖hf1!
This felt good for many reasons.
17...♘b8

18.d4?!
This was the reason why I had castled queenside, and it is definitely not a bad idea, but apparently 18.♘f5+! is kind of winning: after 18...♗xf5 19.♕xf5 ♘bd7 20.♖de1 ♔f8 21.f4 the engine evaluations go through the roof.
Note that White had to wait for ...♘b8; after a premature ♘f5+ ♗xf5 ♕xf5 operation Black would have had ...♘d8!-e6.
18...exd4 19.cxd4
At this point, I started delving more

deeply into the complications after 19...♘bd7 and 19...♘c6!?, and I have to say all I could verify was that White is on the good side of things. I suspected I had been even better at some point, but I wasn't too unhappy with the situation. Time-trouble was looming.

19...♘bd7
I had expected 19...♘c6!? 20.e5 dxe5 21.d5 ♘d4 22.♖xd4 ♗xd4 23.dxe6 fxe6. Here I had calculated 24.♘g4, which is slightly better for White, but the computer prefers another knight move: 24.♘c2!?. White has a safer king and with White now just an exchange down, his material deficit is no longer significant. Black is clearly facing an uphill job.
20.e5!?
I had seen that 20.d5? ♘e5! would favour Black, but interestingly, there was an alternative in 20.h4!?. That

said, the move in the game feels right.
20...dxe5 21.d5 ♕b4!

Fortunately, I had anticipated this move. Black gets to stay in the game due to some nice geometry.

22.♕e2!

Of course 22.dxe6? would allow Black to collect everything with ...♗xe3+ and ...♕xc4xe6, but the most tempting move was 22.♔b1. Fortunately, I had more than one reason to reject it, in particular 22...♗xe3 23.fxe3 ♕xc4 24.♗xf6+ ♘xf6 25.♕xf6+ ♔f8 26.dxe6, and there is an unexpected perpetual mechanism with 26...♕e4+!.

22...♗xh3?

Desperation. Actually, Ding was thinking in the right direction, but this is not exactly the way to do it. 22...♗xe3+ is the most obvious move, but it is the next one that is hard to find. 23.fxe3. Of course, here I only really calculated 23...♘xd5, and I didn't see how exactly Black would save himself in the endgame after 24.♗xd5 ♕c5+ 25.♕c2!. Indeed, that is a lost position for Black. However, instead, Black has a spectacular desperado: 23...♗g4!! (a

truly amazing resource) 24.♗xf6+! (since Black will meet 24.hxg4 with 24...♘e4!) 24...♘xf6 25.hxg4 ♖h4, and Black stays afloat, although according to the engine, the complications are still very promising for White.

23.gxh3 ♔f8 24.h4!

I liked the clever 24.♘c2, but then I realized that the knight belongs on f5. Also, looking at Black's rooks stuck in the corner, I understood that I was probably winning at this point. The material is equal, but I have a safer king and better pieces.

24...♗d4

This was slightly disturbing, since I realized that 25.♘f5 can be met by 25...♗xb2+!. Without too much hesitation, I decided to throw caution to the wind.

25.♖xd4!?

I was lucky that this turned out to be winning, because in truth, I hadn't even seen half the relevant variations. Much cleaner is 25.♗b5!, when White is winning without having to calculate anything, but the problem was that I couldn't resist the exchange sac.

25...exd4 26.♘f5

All of this looks very pretty and works out well. Now 26...♘b6 27.d6! was a beautiful winning line I had calculated while my opponent was thinking.

26...♖xg5!? A classy way to put up some resistance. The immediate 26...♘e5 would lead to the same thing after 27.♗b5, since 27...♖xg5 would be forced either way.

27.hxg5

27...♘e5

I felt that 27...♘e4 was a tougher one to crack.

After 27...♘e4!? 28.♗d3! Black should sacrifice the knight: 28...♘c3!? 29.bxc3 dxc3, and White still has to do some converting. The cleanest would be 30.♔d1! ♛xa4+ 31.♔e1 ♛a1+ 32.♛d1, but I'm not really sure I would have played this. I would probably have gone 30.d6!?, with a winning endgame after 30...♛a3+ 31.♔b1 ♛b3+ 32.♔a1 ♛xa4+ 33.♛a2, but there would still be a long road ahead.

28.♗b5!

The bishop is well positioned here, and it transpires that White is winning after all.

28...♘fg4 29.♔b1!

An attractive move that actually is the only way to win.

29...♔g8?

In serious time-trouble, Ding makes his final mistake, after which the win is in the bag. With 29...♖h2, as he pointed out after the game, he could still have muddied the waters: 30.d6! (this idea, followed by ♖c1-c8+, is quite obvious) 30...cxd6 31.♖c1 ♔g8 (both of us had seen this far, but here the finish wasn't so trivial) 32.♗d3!,

ANALYSIS DIAGRAM

and now (the lines are quite difficult, actually):

– 32...♛b3 runs into 33.g6!, a study-like shot, with the idea of 33...fxg6 34.♗c4+!, followed by ♛e8+ and penetration.

– 32...♘xf2 33.♖c8+ ♔h7 34.♘xd6+ (this little combination is really quite beautiful)

ANALYSIS DIAGRAM

34...♘exd3 35.♖h8+!, and it's mate: 35...♔xh8 36.♛e8+ ♔g7 37.♛xf7+ ♔h8 38.♛f6+ ♔g8 39.♛g6+, with mate on the next move.

– 32...♖xf2 33.♖c8+ ♔h7 34.♘h6+!, when 34...♔g7 35.♖g8 is an incredible mating net. These variations are

possible to find, but you really have to look for them.

30.♘h6+!

Getting rid of the annoying knight construction. The rest is trivial.

30...♘xh6 31.♛xe5 ♘g4 32.♛xc7 Also winning was 32.♛f5, followed by g6. This was just a matter of choice at this point.

32...♔g7 33.g6! Exposing the black king completely. The g4-knight is doomed in all scenarios.

33...♖f8 34.gxf7 d3 35.♖g1 ♖xf7

36.♛c3+ I could probably have calculated a checkmate, but winning the knight forced my opponent's resignation.

■ ■ ■

When Alireza Firouzja beat Ian Nepomniachtchi in that same 7th round, the 19-year-old star could boast a fine double as well, having defeated both world championship finalists in the same tournament. In Round 5, he had emerged victorious from a wildly complicated battle against Ding Liren. When he was asked how it felt to win against the new World Champion, Firouzja quipped that beating Magnus Carlsen is far more difficult. Although it was said in jest, it felt a tad tactless, especially as he had been clearly lost as White at the key moment of the game.

LENNART OOTES

Alireza Firouzja could boast victories over both Ding Liren and Ian Nepomniachtchi. The Frenchman finished shared second after losing a key game to Jan-Krzysztof Duda.

NOTES BY
Jorden van Foreest

Alireza Firouzja
Ding Liren
Bucharest GCT Superbet Chess Classic 2023 (5)
Ruy Lopez, Berlin Defence

1.e4 e5 2.♘f3 ♘c6 3.♗b5 ♘f6
Although Ding Liren's favourite undoubtedly remains the Marshall, like most other top players, he also has the Berlin in his repertoire.
4.d3 ♗c5 5.c3 0-0 6.0-0 d5 7.♘bd2 dxe4 8.dxe4 a5 9.♕c2
A small wrinkle compared to Game 9 of the World Championship match, as Nepo started with 9.a4.
9...♕e7 10.a4

Now, however, via a slightly different move order, the play has transposed to the aforementioned game.

10...♘b8 At first glance, this might seem a bit odd, but it is a typical idea in this line. As the knight is not doing a great job on c6, it is being rerouted to either d7 or a6.
11.h3 Only now does Firouzja deviate from the World Championship game, which saw 11.♖e1 instead.
11...♖d8 12.♗e2

It seems unlikely that this was part of Firouzja's prep, given the time he spent calculating both this and the previous move. Moreover, the engines don't appear to be particularly impressed. Still, the game has only just started, and with all pieces on the board, a complicated struggle lies ahead.

12...♘bd7 13.♖e1 ♘f8
Perhaps not the most accurate move. It might have been better to keep the e5-pawn defended for the moment and make a useful waiting move like 13...h6.

14.♘b3
Firouzja has noticed a clever idea that will secure him the bishop pair. Another option was 14.♘c4, which would also have given him the pair of bishops, albeit through a slightly different sequence.
14.♘c4 forces Black to deal with the attack on the e5-pawn: after 14...♘g6 15.♘xa5 (a little tactic that is quite common in this line) 15...♖xa5 16.b4 White will regain the lost piece and

have some slight pull in the resulting position.

14...♗b6 15.♘fd2

The point behind Firouzja's last move. The other knight is being relocated to c4, where it will put serious pressure on Black's queenside.

15...♗e6 16.♘c4 ♗xc4

The knight cannot be tolerated, and as a result Black must give up the light-squared bishop.

17.♗xc4 ♘e6

This position with the bishop pair seems very pleasant for White. A similar position is often reached from Réti structures. Yet the engines are not all that impressed and evaluate the position as balanced. However, White certainly has good long-term prospects, and Black must play dynamically in order not to end up slightly worse in the long run.

18.g3

A useful strategic move, as it enhances White's dark-square control on the kingside. Furthermore, White intends to slowly improve the position along the lines of ♔g2/♘d2/♘f3.

18...h5

As previously emphasized, Black must aim for dynamic play. His latest decision aligns perfectly with this strategy and is therefore an apt choice.

19.♔g2 h4 20.♕e2

Bringing the queen a bit closer to the defence and preparing to play ♘d2. The immediate 20.♘d2 would have been a grave error due to 20...♕c5, with an immediate win for Black.

20...g6

A serious misstep, since this move severely weakens the black king in the ensuing complications.

It was necessary to involve the

a8-rook in the game by doubling on the d-file: 20...♖d7 21.♘d2 hxg3 22.fxg3 ♘c5!, stopping White from rerouting the knight to f3 just in time. Next Black can play ...♖ad8, when most importantly, the Black's king is a lot safer.

21.♘d2! By rerouting the knight to f3, it becomes a versatile piece that not only protects the white king but also acts as a potent attacker.

21...♘c5 21...♘g5 would have been better, intending to exchange knights after 22.♘f3. But it is understandable that Ding wanted to pressurize the e4-pawn.

CHESS PLAYERS HAVE GREAT MEMORY

"NO WAY WE'LL EVER FORGET OUR WEDDING DAY! TODAY IS BOBBY FISCHER'S BIRTHDAY!"

22.♘f3! Firouzja demonstrates great judgement with his move, wisely discerning that by sacrificing the e4-pawn he will be able to get a formidable attack

22...hxg3 23.fxg3 ♘cxe4

24.♘g5?

As so often in sharp positions, one small misstep can shift the advantage back to the other player. Firouzja's move, while intuitive, allows Black to gain a crucial tempo on White's bishop, enabling him to defend.

Correct was the profound prophylactic move 24.♗a2!, preempting the ...♘d6 defensive resource as played in the game. Black's knight looks impressive on e4, but it is mainly striking at empty air. White, on the other hand, has numerous attacking moves at his disposal, e.g. g3-g4, ♖e1-f1, or ♘f3-g5, which are not easy to prevent. With 24...♗f2 Black manages to pick up a second pawn, but this does not stop White's attack: 25.♖f1 ♗xg3 26.♘g5! ♗f4 (Black has to give up a piece) 27.♘xe4 ♘h5 (Black has lost a piece, but White's attack has been brought to a halt, and now it's the white king that feels unsafe) 28.h4. Another deep move,

the point being that 28...♕xh4 is now met by 29.♖h1. All in all, the position remains incredibly unclear, although the engines have a slight preference for White.

24...♘d6!

This is the defensive idea. The knight defends f7 just in time, but just as importantly, Black gains an important tempo by attacking the c4-bishop.

25.♗a2 ♖e8

Objectively, 25...e4 might have been stronger, but Ding's desire to vacate the d8-square for the other rook is very understandable.

26.h4 Firouzja continues to play as if nothing has happened. Despite White being down a pawn, the game's complexity remains high due to the lingering vulnerability of Black's king.

26.♗f4 is the engine's suggestion, exploiting the fact that Black's queen is pinned down the e-file.

26...♔g7 A good move, stepping out of the a2-g8 diagonal, and overprotecting the f6-knight just in case.

27.♖f1 ♖ad8

The most pragmatic choice by Ding,

which finally activates the only piece that has yet to contribute to the game. However, this move unintentionally provides White with some extraordinary tactical opportunities. The engines propose the nuanced 27...♕d7, setting up for a timely ...♕c6+ check, which should objectively win for Black in the end.

28.♗d2

Firouzja fails to find the correct path ahead, although, in all fairness, it was an exceptionally challenging task to accomplish..

28.h5! is an amazing resource suggested by the engine. The consequences are almost impossible to foresee by the human eye. 28...gxh5 (since 28...♘xh5 runs into 29.♘xf7) 29.♘h7!.

ANALYSIS DIAGRAM

An astounding knight sacrifice! No matter how Black responds, tactics will be unleashed:

– 29...♔xh7 leaves the h5-pawn protected, but now the f6-knight will come under a nasty pin: 30.♗g5 ♘de4 31.♗b1 (one pin follows another) 31...♔g7 32.♗xe4 ♘xe4 (only a temporary queen sacrifice) 33.♗xe7 ♖d2 34.♕xd2 ♘xd2 35.♖fd1. Black might still be slightly better here after either 35...♗e3 or 35...♘b3, but it was still White's best way to continue the game.

– After 29...♘xh7 30.♕xh5 ♔h8 31.♖h1 f6 32.♕g6 Black is up a piece, but it is clear that the position is incredibly dangerous for him. Black's best option is to force a draw in one way or another, e.g. 32...♖g8 33.♖xh7+ ♕xh7 34.♕xf6+ ♕g7

35.♕h4+ ♕h7 36.♕f6+.
28...e4 29.♗f4 e3 30.♖ad1

The critical position of the game has been reached.

30...♘fe4?

At this crucial point, Ding chooses the right square but the wrong piece, which dramatically alters the course of the game. Placing the other knight on e4 would have given Black a winning position. The text-move allows White to get back into the game through a series of forced moves.

30...♘de4! was the way to go. It is certainly not easy to understand that Black can simply leave the f7-pawn unprotected here. As it turns out, it is White's king rather than Black's that will be the most vulnerable: 31.♘xf7 ♖xd1 32.♖xd1 ♘f2!, generating dual threats of either ...♕e4+ or ...♕d7-♕h3+, both with checkmating ideas. White is unable to parry both of them, and should succumb sooner or later.

31.♗xd6 ♘xd6 32.♗xf7

This is even more accurate than capturing with the knight on f7, as will become apparent in a few moves.

32...♘xf7 33.♖xf7+ ♕xf7 34.♘xf7 ♖xd1 35.♕xd1

'Ding chooses the right square but the wrong piece, which dramatically alters the course of the game'

35...♔xf7

Perhaps, when playing his 30th move, Ding had been counting on 35...e2. But: 36.♕d7 is cold shower! All of a sudden, White is playing for mate: 36...e1♕. If White had captured with the knight on move 32, there would be no win here, but now there is: 37.♘e5+!. Black will be swiftly mated in all variations, e.g.: 37...♔h6 38.♘g4+ ♔h5 39.♕h7+ ♔xg4 40.♕xg6, mate.

36.♕e2

36...♔e7?

Another inexplicable mistake, which I just don't know how to explain other than by saying that Ding had simply played too much high-intensity chess over the last few months.

Black could have maintained reasonable chances for a draw by opting for a sensible move like 36...♔g7, followed by 37.♔f1 ♗c5 (the bishop is rerouting itself to the better d6-square) 38.♔e1 ♖e5!, another accurate move, ensuring that Black is ready to meet 39.♕g4 with 39...e2 and protect the rook with ...♗d6. Objectively, the position is simply a draw.

37.♔f1 ♖f8+ 38.♔e1

Given the king's unfortunate position on e7, Black's prospects of salvation have virtually disappeared. Firouzja proceeds to conclude the game with impeccable precision.

38...♖f2 39.♕g4 ♔f6 40.♕g5+ ♔f7 41.♕d5+ ♔f6 42.g4 ♖xb2 43.g5+ ♔e7 44.♕e5+ ♔d7 45.♕g7+ ♔d6 46.♕xg6+

With the g6-pawn gone, White's g- and h-pawns will walk themselves to promotion.

46...♔e5 47.♕e8+ ♔f4 48.g6 ♖b1+ 49.♔e2 ♖b2+ 50.♔d3 ♖d2+ 51.♔c4 ♖g2 52.♕f7+

And Black resigned.

∎ ∎ ∎

Alireza Firouzja and his older brother Mohammadreza, dressed to the nines for the prize-giving. Not for the first time Alireza attracted attention with his shoes (matching nicely with the shirt).

The fight for first place was tense, and the differences were small. Typically, the top four finishers all remained unbeaten. The number of insipid draws was small. There were games in which it was clear that neither player objected to a draw, but even then they had to show some creativity. Since draw offers were not allowed, the players had to find move repetitions.

Firouzja was the only player of the four that finished half a point behind the winner, who hadn't gone undefeated. He had even lost two games. In the first round, he lost to Wesley So, who had his revenge for an unfortunate loss to Firouzja last year that had cost him victory in the Sinquefield Cup and as a result overall first place in the Tour.

Unshaken, Firouzja fought back after this false start and after seven rounds he was in the lead together with Fabiano Caruana. Combative as ever, the fashionista (particularly his shoes attracted attention) shunned a draw early on in his next game against Jan-Krzysztof Duda, only to pay for it dearly with a loss.

With one more game to play, Caruana entered the final round half a point ahead of the chasing pack, which proved enough for tournament victory. All games ended in draws, with the exception of Ding Liren, who finished on a consolatory note, as he comfortably outplayed local favourite Bogdan-Daniel Deac with the black pieces.

Caruana could have made his life easier and avoided any last-game stress if he had converted a highly promising ending against Firouzja in Round 6, but the way it went there was little for him to regret. His flashiest game was his quick win against Maxime Vachier-Lagrave in the third round.

NOTES BY
Fabiano Caruana

Fabiano Caruana
Maxime Vachier-Lagrave
Bucharest GCT Superbet Chess Classic 2023 (3)
King's Indian Defence

This game was played in the third round, against a very familiar opponent. Maxime and I have played countless games over the years. After two draws in the first two rounds, I really wanted to make my mark in the tournament.
1.d4
I wasn't sure whether Maxime would go for his trusty Grünfeld or the Queen's Gambit Accepted, which he had adopted recently and played in the first round against Ding Liren.
1...♘f6 2.c4 g6
The Grünfeld it is! Maxime has been the main defender of this opening at the top level for well over a decade.

3.h4!?

This modern twist has become very popular in recent years. It is the brainchild of Mike Basman and Simon Williams, and was later refined at the highest level by Alexander Grischuk.
3...♗g7 4.♘c3 0-0
Maxime has of course had a great deal of experience against the 3.h4 variation, e.g. in the Candidates tournament, where he delayed castling against Ding Liren.
5.e4 d6 6.♗e2 c5 7.d5 b5

The Benko treatment! I was not surprised that Maxime went for this, as he had also faced this from the white side against Peter Svidler in the 2021 Sinquefield Cup.
8.cxb5 a6 9.a4 axb5 10.♗xb5 ♗a6
So far, we have been following Maxime's game against Peter, in which White played 11.♗d2. I was aware of the existence of that move, but also knew that it is likely to lead to equality. Therefore, I deviated.
11.♗xa6 ♘xa6 12.♘f3
This position is almost new! Of course, Black has a dream Benko

Gambit, as the pawn on h4 is more a weakness than a strength now. However, a pawn is still a pawn.

12...♕d7 13.0-0

13...♕g4?!

This makes little sense. Black's a6-knight belongs on b4, so he should have placed it there immediately. The g4-square should probably be reserved for Black's knight.

13...♘b4 is stronger, and would probably give Black a decent position.

14.♖e1

Natural and accurate. I spent a significant amount of time understanding the subtleties of this position.

14...♘b4 15.♗g5!

This was what I had foreseen when I played ♖e1. The bishop had nowhere useful to go to, so it will be happy to trade itself off for Black's knight.

15...♘h5?

Maxime decided to go straight for my king, but Black is in no position for such aggressive measures.

I had expected 15...h6 16.♗xf6, and here both of Black's options are insufficient for equality:

– 16...exf6 17.♘b5 (attacking the

'Maxime decided to go straight for my king, but Black is in no position for such aggressive measures'

d6-pawn) 17...♖ad8. White is of course better here, with a pawn advantage and a powerful knight on b5. However, Black has some trumps, and the powerful bishop will provide chances for compensation in the future.

– 16...♗xf6 is met by 17.e5 dxe5 18.♖e4!.

ANALYSIS DIAGRAM

Once I had seen this detail, I was very happy! It is too early to capture on e5 and exchange queens. After 18...f5 19.♕e2! the e5-pawn will fall, but under ideal circumstances for White. Black is in trouble.

16.♗xe7!

The only move I considered. Of course, it was scary to allow Black's knight on f4, but collecting Black's entire central pawn chain was too tempting! It turns

out that the attack does not work out.

16...♘f4 Black threatens mate, but it can be stopped.

17.g3 Otherwise it's mate in one!

17...♖fe8 This is certainly not Black's best chance Black, although at this point I felt Maxime was demoralized that he had allowed ♗xe7.

17...♘h3+ was suggested by the great grandmaster Florin Gheorghiu after the game, but after 18.♔f1!, Black's attack peters out:

ANALYSIS DIAGRAM

18...f5 19.♗xf8 ♖xf8 would potentially be scary, if not for the simple 20.♘h2!, when White trades queens and is up too much material.

17...♘bd3 was what I had mainly considered. Black threatens a mating attack with ...♕h3, and has dangerous ideas of ...♘h3 as well. The move I saw when capturing on e7, and the move that convinced me to go for this, was 18.♘g5!, covering the h3-square and trading queens – a multi-purpose resource! Nevertheless, it remains complex: 18...♕xd1 19.♖axd1 ♘xb2 (now nearly all the pieces on the board are hanging, or potentially hanging. It was rather chaotic to calculate this position) 20.♗xf8 ♔xf8

21.♘b5!. It is crucial to preserve this knight! This is the move Maxime mentioned after the game, and the reason he didn't go for this. After 21...♘xd1 22.gxf4, White will also pick up d6, with a powerful pawn duo in the centre. However, there is still a technical task to be done here.

18.♗xd6

This bishop munches up Black's pawns one by one!

18...♘fd3 19.♖e3 ♘xb2

Black manages to collect a pawn, but remains two pawns down.

20.♕b3! The last important and difficult decision.

20.♕e2? looked very tempting, but allows 20...♗xc3! 21.♖xc3 ♘xa4 22.♖e3, and here White would be completely crushing if not for 22...♘c3!, and the fight continues.

20...♘2d3 21.e5

This felt like the most accurate choice to me, but perhaps it would have been easier to capture the last of Black's central pawns.

21.♗xc5! ♘xc5 22.♕xb4 would give

Maxime Vachier-Lagrave inspects his position. An overoptimistic assessment left the Frenchman with a precarious position that was meticulously taken apart by Fabiano Caruana.

White three extra pawns, and Black would have very little hope left.

21...f5!?

A desperate last try, but a necessary one. Black is going all-in with ...f4 ideas.

22.♘h2 A practical little trick. In case of ...♕d4 I would probably repeat the position, and get one move closer to the time-control.

22...♕h3?!

This gives up any hope of resistance. The queen is not active here, and is likely to get trapped.

I believe Maxime rejected 22...♕d4 due to 23.♖d1, but this would lead to a winning, although not entirely trivial endgame. White can also

repeat with 23.♘f3 ♕g4, and here there are several winning moves. The most clinical one is 24.♕b1!, threatening ♖xd3. 24...f4 is now met by the super-precise 25.♘h2! ♕f5 26.g4!, and ♖xd3 picks up even more material. Black can resign.

23.♘e2

Now White threatens ♖xd3, and if the knight from d3 moves anywhere, ♘f4 traps Black's queen. Maxime resigned.

My first win, and it was followed by an important victory over Ian Nepomniachtchi! Plus-two sufficed to win the first event of the 2023 Grand Chess Tour.

■ ■ ■

Caruana's win capped a strong and super-steady performance. In none of his games had he been worse at any point – no mean feat, given his habit to go for strategies aimed at ultimately winning a tournament. It was always clear that his ambition was to win the Superbet Classic, and

Fabiano Caruana: 'I really felt at the end that Anish was trying to win this tournament'

when we sat down for a talk at the end of the event, I also asked him to comment on the ambitions of his rivals.

'In these tournaments, everyone is very ambitious. All of these guys have won tournaments before, with a few exceptions. There's always a player who is a bit of an underdog, let's say Deac in this tournament, although he is still an ambitious player. Obviously, you have Ding and Ian, who have every reason in the world to be ambitious. Or Anish, who has won Wijk aan Zee. Wesley lost his ambition. At some point I could just feel the drop in his ambition to win. Still trying to win, but... It was probably after his game against Ding, when he realized that he had basically missed a very clear chance to win as Black. Alireza was trying hard, but it just didn't work out for him. Alireza still has that youthful optimism, combined with very strong play. But I felt the pressure from Anish especially, because he beat Ding and he got inspired. I really felt at the end that he was trying to win this tournament.'

With a win against Nepomniachtchi in the last round, Giri would probably have earned a play-off against Caruana for the title. Here's that attempt in his own words.

Notes by Anish Giri photo

NOTES BY
Anish Giri

Anish Giri
Ian Nepomniachtchi
Bucharest GCT Superbet Chess
Classic 2023 (9)
Sicilian Defence, Sveshnikov Variation

1.e4 c5 A big surprise. I knew Ian Nepomniachtchi could have prepared anything, but betting against the Petroff felt stupid.
2.♘f3 e6 3.d4 cxd4 4.♘xd4 ♘f6 5.♘c3 ♘c6

The Four Knights Sicilian is a trendy opening. Curiously enough, Fabiano Caruana faced it twice in a row at the 2021 Candidates tournament, where both Grischuk and I played it against him.

6.♘db5 Transposing to the main line of the Sveshnikov. I recommend this move in Part 3 of my 1.e4 Chessable course, which hasn't come out yet. I usually believe in my recommendations (or rather: I recommend what I believe in), especially when the surprise value is maintained. And why not?
6...d6 7.♗f4 e5 8.♗g5 a6 9.♘a3 b5 10.♘ab1!?

This sub-line is what I have in store for my customers, and I felt it was very fitting in this line. And I got exactly what I was hoping for.
10...♗e7
The usual response.
11.♗xf6 ♗xf6 12.a4 b4 13.♘d5 ♗e6 14.♗c4

White gets a pretty good grip on the d5-square, which is typical for the Sveshnikov. This is a quite harmonious position, the only issue for now being the undeveloped b1-knight.
14...0-0 15.0-0 ♗g5 16.♕d3 ♔h8!?
This was a small surprise. Apparently, the a6-pawn is not really hanging (after 17.♗xa6, both 17...♘d4 and 17...f5 are good for Black), and Black can now prepare ...f5.

17.♘d2
After a long think I realized that this was the way to develop my knight, since 17.c3 f5! would give Black promising play in the centre.
17...♗xd2 18.♕xd2 ♕a5
A quite clever-looking move, but not necessarily very good.
19.c3
A fine, simple move, but a more ambi-

tious option was 19.♕d3. I didn't like ...f5 in various lines, but it never quite works for Black, since it would usually be met by ♘e3!.

19...♕c5 20.♗a2 bxc3 21.bxc3

Keeping the queens on the board was obviously the right decision. Due to various psychological factors, I knew I would probably get chances now.

21...♘a5?!

The knight is not well positioned here, even though it actually ends up on the best possible square.

Instead, 21...♘b8! would have been strong, as my opponent told me afterwards. In that case, Black would probably have had full equality.

22.♖ab1

Black's problem is that ...♘c4 doesn't work in view of ♗xc4 and ♘b6, and

if Black passes a move, then ♖b4! is strong, since the reply ...♘c6 is no longer good here in view of ♖c4!.

22...h6?!

I felt that 22...♕a3! was the only way to try and reach equality here by disrupting White's plans somewhat.

23.♖b4!

I invested some time here, as I realized that I should grab my chance instead of going for 23.h3. Now ...♕a3 is no longer possible.

23...♖ab8

This was a critical moment. Unfortunately, I needed a lot of time to realise this and still played a terrible move. The essence of the position was quite clear. The most natural move would be 24.h3, but 24...♘c6! 25.♖c4 ♕a3!

ANALYSIS DIAGRAM

26.♖xc6 ♖b2 would lead to a position that felt too drawish, even though White would end up with an extra pawn and no risk.

24.♖a1!, the first line of the engine, had also occurred to me, but I had unfortunately overlooked that 24...♖fc8 could be met by 25.♘e7!.

I thought 24.♕d3 was my best bet here, followed by what I considered

Ian Nepomniachtchi tried in vain to withdraw from the Bucharest Classic. Exhausted from the match in Astana, the Russian was unable to bring his A-game.

the forced line, 24...♘c6? 25.♖c4 ♕a3 26.♖xc6 ♕xa2, after which I had pinned my hopes on 27.♘b6!. Having concluded that there was nothing better, I finally went 24.♕d3, only to realize that Black had 24...♕a7!, protecting the a6-pawn.

24.♕d3? ♕a7!

To make matters worse, I now over-looked another move as well.

25.h3?!

I already knew I had ruined every-thing, but thinking that Black would play 24...♘c6, I decided to win half a tempo with 25.h3 ♘c6 26.♖bb1!?. Another surprise awaited me.

25...♘b7!

Another minor blow. With little time left, I realized it was really time to pull the emergency break.

26.a5!

It was hard to give up my winning chances, but luckily I managed to readjust to the new situation. Now I expected the game to peter out into a draw, but Ian started playing very ambitiously, asking some questions and getting me in to minor trouble.

26...♘c5!? Now it is White who has to be accurate to preserve the balance.

NEW IN CHESS

Florin Gheorghiu (79), Romania's strongest player for many years, visited the Bucharest Classic every day.

After 26...♘xa5 27.♖a4 ♖b5 28.♘b4 White won't be too bad, since the game will simplify very quickly.

27.♕e2 ♖b5 28.♖xb5 axb5 29.♕xb5

29...♖b8

29...♖xe4!? was also possible. White should be okay after this, but I didn't quite know how to continue. 30.♕b4 f5! would maintain the tension.

30.♕e2?!

I was quite confident of my ability to hold this slightly worse position. 30.♕c6 ♘xe4 31.♘b4! ♖xa2 32.♕xe4 ♕xa5 33.♖a1 ♗d5 seemed unneces-sary, but I should have continued to calculate here: 34.♕e1! ♕b5 35.♖d1!,

and the draw would probably be easier than in the game. 33.♕d3! is also a clean move in this line.

30...♕xa5 31.♗c4 ♕a3 32.♕f3

Accurate. White is okay, but Black can exert some pressure, especially given the time situation and the fact that he is in no danger at all at this point.

32...♔h7

A typical attempt to try and exploit the time situation.

33.♖e1

Not falling for 33.♖d1?! ♕a4 34.♕e2 ♖b2!. More accurate, however, was 33. ♔h2!.

33...♖b2 After 33...♖b2 I calcu-lated a beautiful variation: 34.♘e7 ♗xc4 (actually, 34...♕a8! keeps some pressure) 35.♕f5+ g6 36.♕c8 ♔g7 37.♕g8+ ♔f6 38.♕d8, and Black has to repeat with 38...♔g7.

34.♖d1!

Now I felt I should really be okay, since Black is unable to exert much pressure, since 34...♕c2 can be met by 35.♘b4!.

34...♖a8

A good try, I guess. I had anticipated 34...♖d8, but then, after 35.♔h2 (I intended 35.h4!?, which was also decent), it is not clear how to put pressure on White.

35.♘e3

I had seen the ensuing endgame, which, although slightly unpleasant, was obviously drawn.

I had missed 35.♘c7!?, which leads to some complications.

35...♖a1 36.♗xe6 fxe6 37.♘c4 ♖xd1+ 38.♕xd1 ♕xc3 39.♘xd6 ♘d3

All forced so far. Now I just had to make one more move before the time-control, but I realized things still weren't going to be easy.
40.♘e8! A good move.
40...♕d4

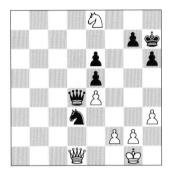

And I got a lot of time added to my clock. Interestingly, I saw the two right moves, but seeing that in both cases I would have to suffer down a pawn, I somehow convinced myself to go for an absolutely insane defensive setup.
41.♕e2?!
A very dumb decision. To make things worse, I had also missed the ...♕d8-♕g5 idea.
The first move that comes to mind is 41.♕f3!, which also draws easily: 41...♘f4 42.h4! (not 42.♔h2 ♕d7 43.g3 ♘g6!, trapping the knight) 42...♕d7 43.g3 ♘g6 44.h5 (I saw this idea, but the pawn count didn't look good. I am also not sure if I would have spotted 44...♖h8 45.♕f8, though I assume this wasn't going to be an issue) 44...♕xe8 45.hxg6+ ♕xg6. It was quite insane to dismiss this endgame in favour of the game continuation. Of course this is quite tenable.

I was about to play 41.♕c2!?, which would indeed be a draw: 41...♕xe4 42.♘c7. Then I noticed 42...♔g8!. Now White has to suffer a bit: 43.♘xe6 ♕xg2+ 44.♔xg2 ♘e1+ 45.♔g3 ♘xc2 (it is ridiculous not to go for this, but I guess I was too arrogant, and perhaps a bit tired at this point as well) 46.♘c5 ♔f7 47.f4, and two against one should be perfectly tenable.
41...♘f4 42.♕c2

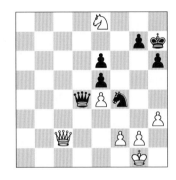

42...♕a1+
I had expected what Nepo is going for here, and it almost brought him victory, so perhaps I shouldn't criticize this.
Instead, 42...♕d8! would have won a pawn: 43.♘c7 ♕g5. White can still hold this, of course, but it would be exactly what I had feared. Therefore, 41.♕f3 or 41.♕c2 would have been a far better ways to suffer.
43.♔h2 ♕f1 44.f3

The whole point of my defensive set-up is that 44...♘e2 can be met by the elegant 45.♕c5!. I thought Black had no way to make progress here and that this would be a relatively easy fortress. This was a bit over-

optimistic, but it did turn out to be a draw.
44...h5 45.♘d6 ♕e1

46.♘b5?! Again, not going for the most obvious move and again a terrible judgement call.
Of course I had planned 46.♘f7, but then I noticed a tactical trick: 46...♘e2 47.♕c5 ♕g3+ 48.♔h1 ♘f4 49.♕c2 ♘xh3. I must have seen that 50.♘xe5! was possible, but I probably felt that it was going to lose. It actually doesn't, and it wasn't exactly rocket science to find this out.
46...h4

47.♘d6? And now White is just lost. On general grounds I had to go to c7, simply because it keeps an eye on the e6-pawn. I didn't see how I could lose after these moves and I think I went for the d6-square almost randomly – and maybe also because I was still hoping to attack the e5-pawn at some point.
47.♘c7 keeps the fortress alive, although things are getting quite nasty, as Black has some ideas here, for example advancing his king via g5-f4, or trap my knight. After 47...♕e3 48.♕b2 ♔g6 49.♕c2 ♕b6

White would have to be very resilient not to lose.

47...♘e2 48.♕c5

48...♘g3?

Giving away the win. After the quiet ...♕g3+−♕f4! manoeuvre the white queen would have been unable to reach the back rank and stop an otherwise inevitable checkmate. This feels very unfortunate.

After 48...♕g3+! 49.♔h1 ♕f4 the threat is not immediately obvious, but it is there. After, for example, 50.♘c8 Black wins with 50...♘g3+ 51.♔g1 ♕d2! 52.♔h2 ♘f1+! 53.♔g1 ♘e3, followed by checkmate on g2. There is just no defence for White.

49.♕g1 Now White has consolidated somewhat again.

49...♘f1+ 50.♔h1 ♕c1 51.♘b7

The knight is barely hanging in there. Now ♘c5xe6 is an idea.

51...♘g3+ 52.♔h2 ♕f4 53.♕b1

Somewhat lucky that the black king is on h7, allowing White to do this.

53...♔h6 54.♔g1 I survived this direct assault on my king.

54...♕d2 55.♔h2 White has few options here, but it is up to Black to try and find a way forward.

55...♘e2 56.♕a1 This or 56.♔h1 were the only two options.

56...♕f4+ After 56...♘f4 White is hanging by a thread, as my knight is about to get trapped: 57.♕g1 ♔h5 58.♔h1 ♕b4 59.♘c5 ♘e2 60.♘d3 ♕b3 61.♘c1 ♘g3+ 62.♔h2 ♕c2 63.♕e1. Miraculously, White keeps everything together. Black can go ...♘h5-f4xg2 here, but this doesn't necessarily win the game.

57.♔h1 ♘g3+ 58.♔g1 ♕e3+ 59.♔h2

59...♕b6? This move ruins it all. My opponent told me afterwards that his idea was to meet ♘a5 with ...♕b5, sidelining the knight. He had missed the check with which I could regain my piece coordination and easily save the draw. Up to this point, White's position had been critical and extremely difficult to hold it, as Black has ideas of catching the knight, and perhaps also of trying to bring the king in via g5 and f4. I was also wondering about ...♘e2-d4 ideas.

All in all, White was in a very bad spot until this huge mistake let me off the hook.

60.♕c1+ ♔h7

61.♘c5 As soon as I made this move, I realized that 61.♕g5 would have drawn on the spot, but luckily it was good enough, too.

61...♘e2 62.♕e1 ♘g3 63.♘d3 ♕b5 64.♘f2

White is no longer worse, so we repeated the moves.

64...♘f1+ 65.♔g1 ♘g3 66.♔h2 ♘f1+ 67.♔g1 ♘g3

I briefly considered whether 68.♔h1 would give me some chances, but it really didn't, the easiest reply being 68...♕e2, with a drawn knight ending.

68.♔h2 Draw.

■ ■ ■

When he was interviewed on Romanian television, Caruana said that he was happy to win the Superbet Classic, but that he still enjoyed rapid chess more – a remarkable statement after winning a fine classical tournament, I thought, and one I asked him to elaborate on.

	Bucharest Superbet Chess Classic 2023				1	2	3	4	5	6	7	8	9	10		TPR
1	Fabiano Caruana	IGM	USA	2764	*	½	½	½	½	½	1	½	1	½	5½	2836
2	Wesley So	IGM	USA	2760	½	*	½	½	1	½	½	½	½	½	5	2799
3	Richard Rapport	IGM	ROU	2745	½	½	*	½	½	1	½	½	½	½	5	2801
4	Anish Giri	IGM	NED	2768	½	½	½	*	½	½	½	1	½	½	5	2798
5	Alireza Firouzja	IGM	FRA	2785	½	0	½	½	*	0	½	1	1	1	5	2796
6	Jan-Krzysztof Duda	IGM	POL	2724	½	½	0	½	1	*	½	½	½	½	4½	2760
7	Maxime Vachier-Lagrave	IGM	FRA	2741	0	½	½	½	½	½	*	½	1	½	4½	2758
8	Ding Liren	IGM	CHN	2788	½	½	½	0	0	½	½	*	½	1	4	2710
9	Ian Nepomniachtchi	IGM	RUS	2795	0	½	½	½	0	½	0	½	*	1	3½	2672
10	Bogdan-Daniel Deac	IGM	ROU	2700	½	½	½	½	0	½	½	0	0	*	3	2638

A delighted Fabiano Caruana with the $100,000 'winner's cheque' together with Grand Chess Tour Executive Director Michael Khodarkovsky, Augusta Dragic, President of the Superbet Foundation, and GM Cristian Chirila.

'My preference for rapid and blitz is very similar to Magnus's preference for rapid and blitz. Preparation at the moment is very demanding work. The amount of work you need to do to get even the slightest chance to play for a win is pretty extraordinary. It's very tiring. And there's times when I enjoy the work – like during this tournament I was working hard

blitz it's basically a non-factor. That's why Magnus prefers it and if you'd ask many players they'd say the same thing.'

Another hot issue is the situation around the world championship, which feels undesirable. How can the chess world be made whole again?

'To get Magnus to play the world championship match again. A mix

think that one player, no matter how strong, no matter if they are number one in the world, should be demanding changes to the format. Do people still want to watch two people playing for the world championship? I think most people still do, just because the title and everything around it is a very high-stakes thing. No matter who wins the world championship, Magnus is the number one in the world, and we accept that Magnus is a better player than Ding, or Ian or me or any other player in the world. But still, being the World Champion carries weight. For instance, Kramnik beat Kasparov, and Kasparov had better results after that; he was the higher-rated player, but Kramnik won the world championship, so he was the World Champion. We haven't always had the consistency of the number one in the world being the World Champion. I don't think that is necessarily a problem. I think it was worse when we basically had a split – when there was confusion about who was the actual World Champion.' ∎

'You're trying to draw water from a stone basically, everything has become much narrower for classical chess'

and enjoying it – but there are times when you don't, and then it's just tedious and boring. You're trying to draw water from a stone basically, everything has become much narrower for classical chess. And for rapid chess it's the opposite – you always get a game. There's still the preparation aspect, but it's pure chess. Preparation rarely decides a rapid match or rapid tournament. And in

of classical, rapid and blitz would probably interest him. And probably shorter and less classical. The thing is that I don't think we should be catering to the preferences of one player, or even a few players. We certainly shouldn't be changing the system because Magnus wants it, even if I agree that the changes that he would want would probably improve things. On principle I don't

Ding Liren:

'Sometimes I can play very, very good chess'

With his adventurous and uncompromising chess – not to mention his unorthodox frankness at the press conferences in Astana – Ding Liren won the hearts of countless chess fans. In Bucharest, the new World Champion looked back on a life-changing experience. He speaks about his ambitions and about his fears in a life outside his comfort zone. In passing, he reveals the name of the other grandmaster who was helping him besides Richard Rapport.

by DIRK JAN TEN GEUZENDAM

It's safe to say that Ding Liren would rather not speak to the press. Throughout his career, China's best chess player has cherished his privacy and feels most comfortable when he is left to his own devices. These days, he realizes that this is no longer an option. If you play for the world championship and win the highest title in chess, you cannot remain silent.

His decision to embrace these new circumstances with an open mind has been a blessing, not only for journalists but also for chess fans. Suddenly they became privy to the thoughts of one of the most brilliant and enigmatic stars of the game. The frankness and honesty with which Ding (30) answered questions at the press conferences during the world championship match almost turned these gatherings into cult events. No matter how stale or unimaginative many of the questions were, Ding would deliver. He rarely dodged questions and always tried to be sincere, even if it meant giving away what many of his colleagues would have considered secrets.

Ding's only concern was that he did not always manage to say exactly what he wanted to say. As I followed the press conferences in Astana, I often wondered how frustrated he must have been. I knew how important he finds it to be precise. Last January, on one of the free days of the Tata Steel tournament in Wijk aan Zee, I had spent an afternoon with Ding Liren in Amsterdam. He wanted to go to a museum and there was a silent understanding that we would not talk about the forth-coming match for the world title. The museum we went to was the Rijks-museum, which houses a magnificent collection of 17th Dutch century paintings. We talked about art and history, and each time Ding failed to find the right word to express what he wanted to say, he would take out his phone and search till he had found it. Although this sometimes resulted in slightly awkward pauses, I was greatly impressed by his uncompromising search for the exact word.

At the Superbet Classic in Bucharest, Ding was mainly exhausted, having arrived straight from Astana, but he stoically underwent the welcome extended to the new World Champion. After the games he had to work his way through a crowd of autograph hunters, and on the

'After the experience of the world championship, any other tournament seems to be less interesting'

first day there was a press conference for local journalists. The new champion tried his best, but there was little worth remembering, with the possible exception of his reaction to the question of whether he had any sports heroes. Ding answered that he liked underdogs, but when he was pressed to come up with examples, he could not think of one. The subject resurfaced when he was asked about his poor performance in Wijk aan Zee that had cost him precious Elo points. Ding happily explained that this had been perfectly fine with him. This loss had caused his rating to drop below Nepo's rating, which made him the underdog in the match!

Ding's main ambition in Bucharest seemed to be to reach the end of the first leg of the Champions Chess Tour without too much damage and then finally go home to China. We had agreed to meet and talk after the final round, and I could only hope that his mood would not be too low by then. It wasn't, because to everyone's relief he won a smooth game against Bogdan-Daniel Deac with the black pieces in that final round.

An hour later he arrives with a smile and we find a quiet room on the second floor of the Grand Hotel Bucharest.

How did you feel when you came here?
'I felt pretty relaxed, because the city is quite warm and there was some rain. After such a long and tough match it's like a vacation. Actually, if I could have chosen, I would have preferred not to play, but I had already agreed to play, so I decided to play this leg and withdraw from the next one in Warsaw.

'Now I will go home and meet my friends, because only a limited number of people could come to Astana. My team could only have seven members. There were Xu Jun, Abigail Tian and Cindy of the chess federation, Rapport and his wife, and me and my mother. And I was in touch with two friends. One of them was also a second. He gave me some technical advice. The openings were mainly prepared by Rapport, but there was also someone else, but I don't want to reveal his name just yet.'

That was Wei Yi?
'No, with Wei Yi I played several training games before I went to Astana. Rapid and blitz. Training games to test my openings, to see how he would react if he saw the position for the first time. Against him I tested this rook a2, for instance [9.♖a2, as he played in the eventful eighth game – see New In Chess 2023/3, pp. 24 ff. – DJtG]. Surprisingly, he reacted quite quickly by playing queen a5, and not b6, bishop a6, the most natural way to answer, right? That had been my reply against Rapport in our training game on Lichess [and also the manoeuvre Nepomniachtchi went for in Game 8 – DJtG] that everybody saw (laughs). Wei Yi played his move quite quickly. After the game I asked him, did you know about this? He said, no, no. But his logic was that I must have prepared something against the most natural way of playing – b6 and bishop a6 – so he deviated from it! (laughs) He played queen a5 because he knew it was one of the moves, although not exactly in this position, but in a similar pawn structure. That was quite funny.'

You came here relaxed, but you also played your first tournament as World Champion. At some point you were at

As might have been expected, the encounter between Ding Liren and Richard Rapport in Round 8 of the Bucharest Classic was a bloodless affair that soon ended in a draw.

the bottom of the rankings. That must not have made you happy as a chess player.

'Recently I have really struggled with my emotions. Here I spent little time preparing before the round. And the results turned out to be quite bad, and also the quality was very, very low. But it didn't bother me much. Because the match was so exhausting. I was not very ambitious in this tournament.'

In Wijk aan Zee you said, the moment I heard about the match I lost interest in the tournament. Was it similar here, that you found it difficult to motivate yourself?

'Yes, after the experience of the world championship, any other tournament seems to be less interesting (laughs). I also missed the big rest room area (keeps laughing) where I could take a walk, where I could rest and sit on the sofa watching the games. Here I had to share the rest room with the others.'

Was it nevertheless painful to play badly?

'Not so much. Yesterday, before the last game my heart was already back in China. I had already left the tournament. Here I played not very professionally – more like an amateur.'

The openings were mainly prepared by Richard Rapport. How or when did you find out that he was perfectly suited to you?

'(Thinks briefly) Well, I will reveal the other second. He's also very important. How to say? OK, because he told me it is better to reveal his name. It was Vakhidov from Uzbekistan. There is Vokhidov and Vakhidov, this is Jakhondir Vakhidov. So I had two grandmasters preparing for me. He was working from Uzbekistan and sent me the lines. We met in Wijk aan Zee [where Vakhidov accompanied his young countryman Javokhir Sindarov, who played in the Chal-

Jakhondir Vakhidov, a member of the Uzbek team that sensationally won the last Olympiad, turns out to have been Ding Liren's secret other second.

lengers –DJtG]. So actually, I found both my seconds in Wijk aan Zee!'

You only decided then?

'I spoke to Vakhidov after the closing dinner. And I asked Rapport to accompany me to Astana after I got back to China. First we had played many training games... on Lichess! (laughs). So Wijk aan Zee was quite a unique experience. I met two seconds there and they helped me a lot.'

Had you been friends with Richard before?

'Yes, we had talked several times. I remember once at the Candidates (in Madrid), after the round in which we drew we had a short conversation

'I will reveal the other second. It was Jakhondir Vakhidov from Uzbekistan'

in the taxi. I asked him, why are you so interested in online tournaments in China? Because I had noticed that he seldom plays the Champions Tour or the chess.com tournaments. But he played many times in Wenzhou online, and he also played many times in Shenzhen online events and I was quite surprised.'

And why was it?
'(Thinks briefly) I forgot!'

It looks like a very natural fit. Both you and Richard very much like to stick to yourself and often work alone. I remember asking both of you at some point who you worked with and both of you saying, With no one!

'Yes, we mainly rely on ourselves. He told me he only had his wife essentially to accompany him, and I didn't have anyone helping me, at least no grandmaster. During the closing ceremony (of the Candidates) we had another brief talk and I found that quite interesting. He asked me if we could play some training games, and I said, OK, we can try. But that was not for the match yet. First I had asked Wei Yi if he could accompany me to Astana, but he had another commitment. So then I thought Rapport was a good choice.'

The start of the match looked terribly chaotic from the outside. You didn't seem to have any control. Was it that dramatic?

'I spoke about that at the press conferences, about the pressure, and I don't want to say much about that now.'

But when you came for the third game, it looked as if something had changed completely.

'First about the opening in the second game [which ended in a painful loss with the white pieces – DJtG], this line should be quite good, this structure. It has been played several times in this tournament with both colours and scored quite well. The opening was OK, so I was beginning to cope with the tournament. I was starting to feel comfortable to be sitting in that chair on the stage.'

Many people were surprised by the way you kept your calm later on, regardless of whether you won or lost a game. Where did you get that flexibility, that resilience?

'I have to give credit to my friends. They supported me quite a lot. I also have to say that recently I have often lost in the first or second rounds, mainly with the white pieces. I remember losing many times. But later, like in the Candidates, I would fight back. Therefore I am not that worried. Because I have that kind of experience.'

Did this coolness also help you in the fourth tie-break game, when you had to decide whether you were going to play for a win? Did you strongly feel that this was your moment?

'No, I didn't take any such decision during this game. It was not a decision to play for a win or play for a draw. It was just a move, and the move played itself (laughs). I just thought that I needed to play this move. I thought I was better, so I had to continue. I cannot recall my

thoughts during the game, but at this point I basically had a choice between rook g6 and king g8, queen d5, rook f7. And I thought, rook g6 is a better way to avoid a check.'

I was watching the live video. When you were playing this, you looked very calm.

'Yes (laughs). But I was not actually all that calm. I was fully focused. I was determined.'

Unlike in Game 7, during which you suddenly froze. What happened there?

'I froze, because I was just too relaxed at that point. I thought the worst was behind me and I could seek for an advantage. I was looking for the best move in the position. I was too relaxed and didn't see the danger of the potential time-trouble. I didn't sense any kind of danger at that point.'

You made a remarkable statement before the match, saying that if you didn't win the match, you might quit chess. Was that serious?

'Not very serious. I guess every chess player has these thoughts of quitting chess at some point. Or sometimes they have all kinds of reasons to want to do other things besides chess. My

thought at that point was that if I lost, then maybe after the Asian Games, which I had already agreed to play, maybe I would retire. But you know, sometimes your thoughts and what you do are different. I am not sure if I would have changed my mind if I had lost.'

There have been so many occasions when players had bad positions and then, afterwards, they'd tell me that at some point they were thinking of resigning. But they never do.

'Yes, yes, during the game there are many thoughts like this (laughs). Once an engineer, a former class mate, asked me, What do you think about when you play chess? And I answered him, about nothing, I totally focus on chess. But that is not always the case.'

You won the title. How much are you enjoying it? What kind of feeling is it?

'(Thinks long) All I can say is that it is better to win than to lose.'

You were mostly afraid of losing...

'I was also afraid of winning the match. Because no one from my circle, from my comfort zone, has done this before. After winning this match I was totally out of my comfort zone. Before the

Ding Liren's unorthodox openness almost turned the press conferences in Astana into cult events.

something completely different. 'Yes, after the last classical game a quote crossed my mind and I mentioned it. I attributed it to Camus, but it was in fact said by the German writer Rilke, Rainer Maria Rilke. It was something I remembered at this critical moment. The quote was: There's no such thing as victory, perseverance is everything.'

What are your expectations when you go home now?
'First there will be a big press conference for many media that will take some two hours. Then I will meet my friends. Also, I don't know, sometimes I feel like I need to see a doctor to see if I have some psychological problem. But I don't know if it's something common among grandmasters.'

What kind of problem do you mean?
'(Seeing my worried look) I am not sure if I have a psychological problem! (Laughs). Maybe I am good. Maybe it's just... After the first two rounds, my friends urged me to make an emergency call to a psychologist in China. So maybe it's better

match I often declined to be interviewed, but now I have to get used to it.'

On the other hand, you became very popular by the way you handled the press conferences. You seemed incapable of avoiding subjects or lying. Why is that?
'(Thinks for a long time) Sometimes I did not know what to say at the press conference and I honestly said what I thought. Now I have more time to think and many answers to choose from. So I can choose between telling the truth and holding on to it. After the game that was not possible.'

Did you get messages from friends advising you not to tell everything?
'No, but the people of the chess federation said that if I wanted to, I could have a translator. But at that point I just wanted to express my own thoughts.'

From our conversation in Amsterdam I know that you like to check your phone to find the right words. You are very careful about what you want to say. But there you could not always find the right word.

'Yeah, yeah. You know, sometimes I want to say something very deep (laughs), so I have to carefully check the words, so as not to mislead others. During the press conference, I sometimes didn't have the time

to check, but I still wanted to say something original. And sometimes I would say quite strange things. Also there were many mistakes. Just like ChatGPT sometimes creates the perfect answer, very careful and very accurate, and sometimes you don't know what it's saying.'

You must have read reports in which you were quoted as saying one thing, whereas in fact you wanted to say

'Sometimes I would say quite strange things. Just like ChatGPT sometimes creates the perfect answer, very careful and very accurate, and sometimes you don't know what it's saying'

to go for a check after I get back to China. I didn't have such an experience before. Maybe it was because of the pressure. Now I feel quite well, maybe because of winning the match or because the match is over. Because chess players are very good at finding explanations why something happened, right? Over the board, like where did you make mistakes or why did you lose the game? But if you try to find reasons away from the board,

CHESSBASE 17

Ding Liren in front of an early self-portrait by Rembrandt during a visit to the Amsterdam Rijksmuseum on a free day of the Tata Steel tournament last January.

that is quite difficult. There are so many reasons.'

You mean that having this title is really something big, and actually creates new problems?
'(Thinks for a long time) Recently I have been reluctant to read news about me on the Internet...'

You want to have your private life...
'Yeah.'

People in China are very proud of you for winning the championship. In the chess world, there are obviously people who are impressed by your achievement, but still point out that there's always Magnus. Yes, you won the championship, but...
'Oh, yes. I know that I didn't have this kind of domination like Magnus. But I will try my best and try to win more trophies in the future.'

Not that long ago, when people were wondering who would be the best opponent for Magnus, your name was one of very few that were mentioned,

and with good reason. Would you like to play a match against him?
'Well, I heard that Argentina wants to organize a rapid and Chess960 match between us at the end of this year. And I can say that I am interested. Let's see.'

Winning the match was a great achievement. What are you most proud of?
'Proud of myself? (Looks a bit puzzled, thinks for a very long time) I don't know whether it's proud or relieved... Let's say proud of making history, proud of winning the world title...'

Winning the title for your country?
'No, actually my goal is to become the best player, not winning the title.'

To be the highest-rated player?
'Not to have the highest rating, but play the best games at some point. That's my goal.'

That would show in your rating. Or do you want to have the feeling for yourself that you are the best player? Is it a feeling?

'Yes, it's a feeling. That somebody says that you played a game like 3000 Elo. That would make me quite happy.'

That you would be the standard. Now it's playing like Carlsen, but then it would be playing like Ding Liren?
'Ah, it's quite hard to be the best player, to get a higher rating than Carlsen. But sometimes I can play very, very good chess.'

You have already done that. You have played many wonderful games.
'Yeah. I remember at one point during Covid... Although I wasn't playing so much over the board, I think that my strength at that time was quite high. Once I played against Nakamura on chess.com, and this was quite a tense match, it was only decided in the Armageddon game. I remember really enjoying that period. Because this was a time when I had a huge interest in chess. I discovered many, many things that I hadn't known before. That's why I said that Covid actually didn't affect me too much, because I used the time to improve my play. I raised my ceiling. Sometimes it's just my job, but somehow I managed to raise my ceiling and then I can play a very, very good game.'

When the interview is over, Ding quickly returns to his room, and I do the same. By coincidence there is a Chinese lady in our elevator – probably a business woman, by her appearance. She observes Ding, and when he gets out on floor 10, she turns to me and asks me whether we are in Bucharest for a meeting. While I try to think of an answer, she quickly adds, 'Because he is a Chinese gentleman'. I say, 'Yes, he is the chess world champion'. When I get out on floor 14 and she proceeds to a higher floor, I hear her repeat to herself as the doors are closing, 'chess world champion'. Her intonation does not suggest a question, but it is clear that he has set her thinking. ∎

Class always tells. Following a protracted break from classical chess, Peter Svidler won the 28th TePe Sigeman tournament. He may have been a bit rusty, and a bit shaky in the openings, but he certainly had not forgotten how to play.

by ERWIN L'AMI

The Return of Peter Svidler

'Veteran' successfully competes with young guns in Malmö

As the president of the Swedish Chess Federation noted in his opening address, the Tepe Sigeman has become a hallmark for Swedish chess. The annual tradition that celebrated its 28th edition saw a small hiatus in the years 2015-16, but repositioned itself firmly on the map again when, in 2017, chess aficionados Joel Eklund, chairman of the oral health company TePe, and Johan Sigeman of law firm Sigeman & Co joined forces. The tournament's solid standing was fittingly underpinned with a festive opening at the Malmö Rådhus, the impressive town hall that was completed in 1547, when Malmö was one of Scandinavia's largest cities.

I counted myself lucky to be there. Together with Swedish Grandmaster Stellan Brynell I had been asked to provide the daily commentary. As such, I had a perfect view of what I thought might be one of the most exciting editions so far.

First and foremost, this had had to do with the participants. The organ-izers stuck to the tried and tested formula of inviting an appealing mix of players: two experienced legends of the game, Peter Svidler and Boris Gelfand, together with a bunch of young guns like Arjun Erigaisi, Dommaraju Gukesh, Vincent Keymer and Abhimanyu Mishra. Add to that the 2021 winner Jorden van Foreest and local favourite Nils Grandelius (a three-time winner!), and exciting chess was virtually guaranteed.

Indeed, the first three rounds saw a 75 per cent win rate and as so often in such relatively short events – those early results largely determined the outcome for most of the players.

Dommaraju Gukesh, the rating favourite, seemed to be particularly eager. The Indian super-talent swiftly defeated Jorden van Foreest in Round 1 and next showed no signs of slowing down when he was paired against his good friend Vincent Keymer in Round 2.

Peter Svidler hadn't played a classical tournament in well over a year.
His openings were patchy, but he nullified that handicap with excellent play.

NOTES BY
Gukesh D

Gukesh D
Vincent Keymer
Malmö TePe Sigeman 2023 (2)
Ruy Lopez, Möller Defence

This was my second game. I had started with a win over Jorden van Foreest as Black, so I was looking to build on the momentum.

1.e4 I decided to stick with 1. e4, which I had played against Vincent Keymer in our previous classical encounter in the WR Masters in Dusseldorf last February.
1...e5 Vincent played the Najdorf in our previous game. I came close to winning, but the game ended in a draw.
2.♘f3 ♘c6 3.♗b5 a6 4.♗a4 ♘f6 5.0-0 ♗c5
This is not his regular opening, but he had played it a few times, so I was ready for it.

Recently, he had had a lot of interesting battles in the lines after 5...♗e7.

6.c3 b5 7.♗b3 d6 8.d4 ♗b6
9.♗e3 Not as popular as the lines with 9.a4, but still a very relevant line, of course.
9...0-0 10.♘bd2 ♖e8 11.h3 h6 12.♕e2!?

This is an interesting novelty that I knew about and that I had checked the morning before the game.
12...♖b8 The first serious think of the game. Vincent had been surprised by ♕e2 and played a natural move after thinking for 10 minutes.
After 12...♗b7, 13.d5 is the point: the structure after 13...♘e7 14.♗xb6 cxb6 is slightly better for White.
There were other accurate replies, 12...♘a5 being one of them.
13.♖ad1 I was still in my prep, as thankfully my trainer had told me at the last minute that 12...♖b8 was possible, the point being that Black can then play 13...♗d7, when after 14.d5, the sequence 14...♘e7 15.♗xb6 ♖xb6 is possible. So I knew that 13.♖ad1 was the move to play.
13...♗d7

Here I was out of my prep, or so I thought... When I checked my notes later, I found this move there.

'I was still in my prep, as thankfully my trainer had told me at the last minute that 12...♖b8 was possible'

14.♗c2 Played after 20 minutes, and it is the best move, because I had to protect the e4-pawn. I had tried to make 14.♖fe1?! work for a while, but to no avail: 14...exd4 15.cxd4 ♘xe4 16.♘xe4 ♖xe4 17.♕c2 ♖e8 18.♗xh6 ♖xe1+ 19.♖xe1 ♘xd4 20.♕g6 ♘xf3+ 21.gxf3 ♕f6, and Black is clearly better.

14...♕c8?!
The start of a dubious, or at least dangerous, plan. It was hard to find a good plan for Black anyway, since the usual approach with 14...exd4 15.cxd4, the knight moves and ...c5 did not work here: 14...exd4 15.cxd4 ♘b4 (15...♘e7 is the comp's idea, but this looks super-dangerous) 16.♗b1 c5 17.dxc5 ♗xc5 18.♖xc5 dxc5 19.e5, with a clear advantage for White;
Maybe the best idea to create some play on the queenside was 14...a5, but having the queen on d8 with the rook on d1 was a bit scary,
15.♖fe1
I don't really think 15...♗xh3 was possible, but in any case, 15.♖fe1 was a useful move, since taking on h3 is out of the question now.

15...♕b7?!
Vincent continues with his plan, but now the queen is really misplaced. The sacrifice clearly didn't work: 15...♗xh3? 16.gxh3 ♕xh3 17.♕f1.

16.a3! I was really happy with this move, as it stops any kind of play on the queenside.
I considered 16.g4, but was not sure about it after 16...b4.
And after 16.♘f1 exd4 17.cxd4 ♘b4! it would become clear why 16.a3 had been a useful move.
16...a5 17.♘f1! Now there is no ...♘b4. **17...a4**
Black controls the queenside, but the attack on the other side will be too strong.
He should have tried 17...exd4 18.cxd4 ♘xe4 19.d5 ♗xe3 20.♘xe3 ♘a7 21.♘d4, even though White would still have been better.
18.♘g3 ♘a5 19.♘h4 ♘c4

20.♗c1 20.♘h5! was stronger, but I didn't even bother to consider this, thinking that ♗c1 was good enough; I considered 20.♗xh6 for a while, but there was no need.
20...d5
I thought that 20...exd4! was his

Gukesh tore away with two wins, but could not keep that pace and finished shared second.
In Round 2, he won a game against Vincent Keymer that he was very pleased about.

only chance: 21.cxd4 c5 22.d5 ♘e5, and I felt that this would give him some chances, but the comp disagrees: 23.♘hf5 ♗xf5 24.♘xf5 ♕d7 25.f4 c4+ 26.♔h2 ♘d3 27.♗xd3 cxd3 28.♕xd3, and White is winning. Best in this line was 22...♖a5! 23.♖f1 ♗d8, the usual comp stuff.

21.♕f3

21...♘d6
21...exd4 was Black's best option, but it would be hard to see Black surviving this line: 22.♗xh6 dxe4 23.♕f4 ♕d5 24.♗xg7 ♕d6! (24...♔xg7 loses to 25.♘gf5+) 25.♕xf6 ♕xf6 26.♗xf6 d3 27.♗xd3 exd3 28.♖xe8+ ♖xe8 29.♖xd3, and White is better.

22.♗xh6!

This looked so convincing that I didn't really calculate the sacrifice to the end.

22...dxe4
Black is also defenceless after 22...♘dxe4 23.♘xe4 ♘xe4 24.♗xe4 dxe4 25.♕g3 g6 26.♘xg6.

23.♕e3 gxh6 24.♕xh6

24...♖e6 There were some nice lines after 24...exd4:
– 25.♕g5+ ♔h7 26.♕xf6 ♕d5 27.cxd4, and White is winning.
– I thought this was easier than 25.♘g6 fxg6 (there is a nice mate after 25...♔h7 26.♘h5 ♗f5 27.♘f6+! ♘xf6 28.♕h8#) 26.♕xg6+ ♔f8 27.♕xf6+ ♘f7 28.♗xe4 (28.♘h5!) 28...♖e6 29.♕xe6 ♗xe6 30.♗xb7 ♖b3, which prompted me to look for something better.

25.♘gf5
When I played this, I had calculated the attack through to the end.

25...♘fe8 25...♘xf5 would lose to 26.♘xf5 ♘e8 27.♕g5+ ♔f8 28.♗xe4 (or 28.♖xe4 ♖g6 29.♕e7+).

26.♕g5+ ♔f8 27.♕h5 ♘xf5

28.♘xf5 Alternatively, 28.♕h8+!? ♔e7 29.♘xf5+ ♔d8 30.♗xe4 should be winning as well.
28...♖g6 29.♗xe4 ♕a7 30.♕h8+ ♖g8 31.♕h6+ ♔g7 32.♘xg7 ♖xg7 33.♖e3 This rook lift wins by force.

33...♗g4
Black will be mated after 33...♔g8 34.♖g3 ♖xg3 35.♕h7+ ♔h8 36.♗g6+ ♔g8 37.♕h7+ ♔f8 38.♕xf7 mate.
34.♖g3 ♗xd4 35.♖xg4
And Black resigned.
Although my opponent did not have his best day overall, I was very happy with this game – I played an interesting novelty that was followed up by accurate moves to gain an advantage, and finished it off with nice calculation.
With this win I took the lead with 2 out of 2, but I kind of lost the thread after this game and finally ended up in shared second place. But I had a lot of fun in Malmö and it was a very well organized event!

■ ■ ■

I should have given a spoiler alert concerning Gukesh's remark about the remainder of this event, but it was oh so true! From his game against Keymer onwards, his tournament seemed to falter – first with a very shaky draw against Nils Grandelius in Round 3, in which Nils threw in a classic Greek gift on h7, followed by an 'accident' in the next round against his fellow-countryman.

Arjun Erigaisi
Gukesh D
TePe Sigeman 2023 (4)

position after 30.♗b3

Although Erigaisi had been better for most of the game – at one point far better, even – Black doesn't seem to have much to worry about in the diagrammed position. Gukesh evidently thought so, too, since he played **30...♘xd5,** to which Arjun replied with **31.♕c6**. At this point **31...♘f4** was the plan, intending to try and trap the queen with 32...♖d6 after 32.♕xh6. Erigaisi had looked deeper, though, and captured on h6 anyway! **32.♕xh6**

It turns out that after 32...♖d6 White can deliver the blow 33.♗xf7+!. Now

33...♔xf7 34.♕h7+ ♔f6 35.♖c7 loses outright, but 33...♖xf7 34.♖xc8! nets White an extra pawn. Note how the rook had to be lured away from f8, ensuring that Black couldn't recapture on d8 after 34...♖xh6 35.♖xd8+.
Amazingly, Gukesh could have escaped with 32...♗xh3!!, the idea being that 33.gxh3 ♖d6 is a much-improved version of the above line – so much improved, in fact, that Black just wins. White has better tries, of course, with 33.♖e5 as probably the most dangerous one. In that case, however, Black would hold after 33...♗xg2+ 34.♔h2 ♘h3!, protecting g5 and preparing ...♖d4-h4. Having missed the ♗xf7+ tactic, and in impending time-trouble, Gukesh failed to find the right sequence and quickly succumbed after:
32...♗f5 33.♖c6 ♖d3 34.♖e5 ♖xb3 35.♖xf5 f6 36.♖xf4! gxf4 37.♕g6+ ♔h8 38.♖c5

Black resigned, as 38...f5 39.♕h6+ ♔g8 40.♖c6 is a mating attack.

This loss didn't mean the end of Gukesh's tournament aspirations, but it had become clear that his initial aura of invincibility was in tatters.

Entirely unnecessary
Someone who did have a great time in Malmö was Abhimanyu Mishra. 14-year-old Abhi holds the record for being the youngest chess player ever to earn the GM-title, but strange as it may sound, he still has a long way to go to the top. I had seen Mishra at work in Wijk aan Zee this year, and felt that the Malmö invitation might have come a bit too early. I worried about his pros-

Abhimanyu Mishra had a great time in Malmö. The 14-year-old was in contention for first place till the very last day when he had to settle for shared second.

pects in this very strong field, but that proved entirely unnecessary! After a draw against Peter Svidler with the black pieces, Abhi struck in the subsequent rounds, boldly taking an early lead. This is what happened in Round 2.

Abhimanyu Mishra
Jorden van Foreest
Malmö TePe Sigeman 2023 (2)

position after 25.♘e3

Jorden had played the opening very enterprisingly and gained a large advantage. In the diagrammed position, though, things are already looking less clear. White wants to recapture on c4, open the position

on the queenside or in the centre, and Black's counter-chances are anything but obvious. The h-file is open, but the king on g1 is clearly not getting mated any time soon. The engine indicates 25...c3 as Black's best bet here, not trying to hold on to the pawn, but to give it back under slightly better circumstances. Jorden's move is more ambitious, but it simply doesn't work.
25...b5 Holding on to the extra pawn, but allowing White to penetrate his position from all sides.
26.axb5 axb5 27.exf5 exf5 28.♖a7 ♖d8 29.d5!

Jorden sank into thought for close to 30 minutes, but it was already too late.

29...c5 A logical attempt to keep the position as closed as possible.
30.d6!
Of course! With one move White clears the d-file for the c1-rook and the d5-square for the knight. Given Abhi's serious time-trouble, the only question remaining was whether White would reach move 40 without doing damage to his own position.
30...♕xd6 31.♘d5 ♖h6 32.♖d1 ♖e6

33.♕c2! Super-precise. 33.♕b2 is tempting, and also what we looked at in the commentary room. The threat is ♘c7+ here, too, but after 33...♔f7 there is no immediate knock-out blow. With the queen on c2, White simply takes on f5.
33...♕e5 34.♘c7+ ♔f8 35.♘xe6+ ♕xe6
Materially speaking, things don't look all that bad for Black, but it's all about the kings here. Black's is very vulnerable, whereas White's is not.
36.♕c3 ♗f6 37.♕d2 ♗d4 38.bxc5 ♗e8 39.♕g5 ♖d7 40.♖xd7 ♕xd7

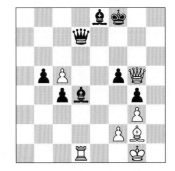

When the players had reached move 40, it had become clear that

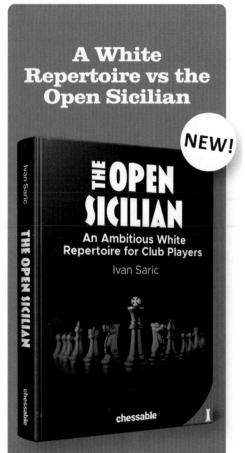
Abhi would win – not with 41.♕d2?, though, since this would be met by 41...c3, after which 42.♕xd4 ♕xd4 43.♖xd4 c2!, allowing the c-pawn to queen. 42.c6 looks like a tempting improvement, but then 42...♗xf2+! would be awkward.

What Mishra played is far simpler:
41.♖e1 ♗f7 42.♕h6+ ♗g7 43.♕f4

Black resigned. Between Black's king and White's c-pawn, the position is too much to handle.

As if that wasn't enough of a dream start for Mishra, look at what happened in Round 3.

Vincent Keymer
Abhimanyu Mishra

position after 24.g5

Vincent had played a model game thus far, and his last move, 24.g5, is already signalling that Black is in dire straits. The most obvious reply, 24...♘d7, loses to 25.♖xd7 ♕xd7 26.♕e5!, with a double attack on b8 and g7, but Abhi had a tricky reply planned – one that causes his opponent to lose the plot.

24...♕b6!?
Suddenly threatening a variety of tactics on squares b2, f3 and d4, with the result that White was unable to capture on f6 just yet.
25.♕e5 ♗xf3 26.♖d6 ♕g1+ 27.♖d1 ♕b6

This led to a rather awkward moment in the commentary room. As Stellan and I were explaining that Vincent had been playing a great game and would now crown it with the neat 28.♖f1! ♗g2 29.♖f2!, Keymer started thinking. We took this as a sign he was simply double-checking things, announced that the win was imminent and moved on to the other games. Shortly thereafter, we were dragged back in when, instead, the game continued
28.♖d3 ♕g1+ 29.♗d1 ♖c8

and suddenly things aren't clear at all. What's more, with time-trouble on the way, the position had become very hard to play for White. The first thing to look at now is 30.gxf6 ♗xd1 31.♖g3, but the simple 31...♕f1 32.♖xg7+ ♔h8 gives Black a completely winning game, as the bishop will head back to g6 via h5.

The engine indicates 30.♔c1 as the saving move, but Vincent had missed Black's 30th move.

30.♕c7 ♖e8! 30...♖f8 31.♖d8 ♘e8 32.♕e7! was the point at which 32...♗xd1 33.♕xf8+! ♔xf8 34.♗a3+ would lead to mate. After the game continuation, White is completely lost. **31.♖d2 ♗xd1 32.gxf6 ♗h5+ 33.♔c1 ♗g6+ 34.♔b2 gxf6**

Black has two extra pawns, and, more importantly, a strong initiative owing to the opposite-coloured bishops. Vincent played on for a while but eventually had to resign (0-1, 55).

Keymer failed to get back in the tournament and even dropped under the coveted 2700 rating barrier. Given his immense potential, I have little doubt that this setback will be of a temporary nature.

The same goes for Arjun Erigaisi who, to me, is very hard to define as a player stylistically. He is certainly very ambitious, which also shone through in his opening preparation. In Malmö he had a few uncharacteristic lapses. Take the following fragment from his game against Jorden van Foreest, in Round 5.

Jorden van Foreest
Arjun Erigaisi
Malmö TePe Sigeman 2023 (5)

position after 47.♖f6

White's last move, 47.♖a6-f6, can easily be parried with 47...♔g7, when it's not readily apparent what White could still do to improve his position. In the commentary room, Jorden later showed the line 48.♖h4 ♖xg2 49.♔g5, which looks a bit scary; but he pointed out that 49...♖h2 50.♖xg6+ ♔h8 should easily do the job. The g-pawn provides plenty of counterplay. Instead, Arjun spent 14 seconds(!) on **47...♔g8,** when **48.e6 ♖xe6 49.♖exe6 fxe6 50.♖xf8+!** led to a winning pawn ending. Arjun had only counted on 50.♖xg6+ ♔f7 51.♖xg4, with a worse but quite tenable endgame. As it happened, after **50...♔xf8 51.♔xg4** he resigned. Black will be in zugzwang after 51...♔f7 52.♔g5 ♔g7 53.g3 ♔f7 54.♔h6 ♔f6 55.g4 ♔f7 56.g5.

Nils Grandelius also took advantage of a hiccup by Erigaisi.

Arjun Erigaisi
Nils Grandelius
Malmö TePe Sigeman 2023 (2)

position after 19.♖g5

In this position, Nils gained a decisive advantage with **19...♕b6!** Threatening both checkmate on b2 and – after, for instance, 20.b3 – 20...♕e3+ 21.♕xe3 ♘xe3, winning material. Erigaisi tried to muddy the waters with **20.♖xg7+** but Nils refused to let this one slip.

These results made it impossible for Arjun to fight for first place this year. Meanwhile, Nils rose to +1 in the standings, and after his recent win in Reykjavik he seems to be on a high again.

Arjun Erigaisi was ambitious as ever, but lost two games, one of them against local favourite Nils Grandelius.

Like Mishra, Peter Svidler scored back-to-back wins in Rounds 2 and 3. This obviously laid the foundations for the remainder of his event. Peter hadn't played a classical tournament in well over a year, and it's testament to his stature that he still performed the way he did. Although, I would say with a distinct touch of understatement, not particularly well prepared with regard to the opening, Peter managed to nullify this handicap with excellent play. In Round 2, against Gelfand, in particular, it certainly looked as if he wasn't going to survive the first 15 moves. But he definitely did, and here he shows you how.

NOTES BY
Peter Svidler

Boris Gelfand
Peter Svidler
Malmö TePe Sigeman 2023 (2)
King's Indian Defence

This being my first classical tournament since the 2021 Grand Swiss, I had a customary (somewhat intentional) quiet first round game vs Mishra, and then had the fun assignment of preparing for a black game vs Boris Gelfand. I've been facing that task for far longer than most of the field of the TePe Sigeman 2023 have been alive, and yet I tend to fail at it. And so it came to pass.
1.♘f3
I was ready to play 1.d4 ♘f6 2.c4 d6, so this move is giving me an out – I could still play 1...c5 here; or anything, really.
1...♘f6 2.c4 d6

'I've been facing the task of preparing for Boris for far longer than most of the players in Malmö have been alive'

But no, I was pretty set on this idea, having noticed that Boris appears to dislike allowing the 3.♘c3 e5 4.d4 e4 lines, meaning I was very likely to get ...
3.d4 g6 4.♘c3 ♗f5
... this position, in which he has been playing 5.d5 fairly consistently in recent years. Black isn't doing all that great there, either, but at least I had some kind of an idea.
5.♕b3 Not here, though.
5...♕c8 6.h3!

There is really no excuse I can offer for not looking at this before the game. This is far from a novelty, and the engines love it, too.
6...c6?! There aren't any good choices as such, but this is a little bit too artificial.
6...♗g7 7.g4 ♗d7 8.e4 0-0 9.♗e3 is pretty bad, too – but at least the black pieces don't get in the way of each other as much.
7.g4 ♗e6 I went for this with some vague dreams of creating enough of a distraction by hinting at ...b7-b5 to maybe deter Boris from the most straightforward development, but it was never going to be a realistic proposition.
8.e4

8...♗g7
8...b5 makes sense – we badly want to trade some pieces, and eliminating parts of White's gorgeous centre is extremely important, too; but it just doesn't work tactically: 9.♘g5! ♗xc4 (no choice, otherwise the position just crumbles) 10.♗xc4 bxc4 11.♕xc4, and the weakness on f7, combined with a general lack of development, should decide the game fairly soon.
9.♘g5!
A very nice move, making sure ...b5 is unplayable and preparing to grab more space with f4.
9...c5
An incredibly ugly choice, but I couldn't see any way to not play this. Lines like 9...0-0 10.f4 ♘a6 11.e5 ♘e8 12.♗g2 seemed worse.

10.♘xe6?!
This still gives White a massive edge, but I was much more worried about 10.d5 ♗d7 11.f4, after which I was genuinely fearful of not making it to move 20. My plan was to play 11...h5 12.e5 ♘h7, hoping to at least make a mess of it, but after the simple 13.exd6! ♘xg5 14.fxg5 exd6 15.♗f4 Black's position will start collapsing.
10...fxe6 11.d5 0-0

Black is still in a lot of trouble, but at least I could now hope to fight for some dark-square control.

12.♗e3

The quiet 12.♗g2 ♘a6 13.0-0 ♘c7 14.a4 leaves Black with very little counterplay, since trying to open things up with ...exd5 and ...e6 is very likely to result in White's edge increasing dramatically due to his bishops getting much more operational freedom.

12...♘fd7!?

I felt as if I couldn't wait quietly for White to improve, and decided to try and get the bishop to d4 asap.

13.f4

Still fine, but based on a miscalculation. After 13.♗e2 ♗d4 14.♘b5 e5 White would have the very important additional resource of 15.g5!, aiming to put the bishop on g4, while Black, apart from a very nice ♗d4, doesn't have much at all to write home about.

13...♗d4

Boris played 13.f4, thinking 13...♗d4 is impossible due to 14.dxe6.

14.♘b5?!

But having realized that after 14.dxe6 I can reply with 14...♘b6! (14...♗xe3? 15.♘d5) 15.♗d2 ♛xe6, he lost track

Peter Svidler and Boris Gelfand have eaten quite a bit of salt together and their game was bound to be exciting. Svidler prevailed when Gelfand collapsed in time trouble.

a bit and failed to consider the move I was most worried about: 14.♗d2!, after which Black still struggles to generate counterplay. I wanted to play 14...♘f6, but Black is in a lot of trouble after both 15.♗d3 and 15.0-0-0!?, finishing White's development and inviting Black to open some files for the white pieces by grabbing the e4-pawn with 15...♗xc3.

14...e5 15.f5 a6

Since 16.♘a3 doesn't look all that hot, we're at least forcing White to give us a protected passer on d4– and perhaps even more importantly, some squares for our knights.

16.♘xd4

16...exd4

Giving myself the e5-square for the knights, which makes the kingside a bit more defended, at least optically. My original plan was 16...cxd4 17.♗h6 a5!?. I felt as if I absolutely didn't care about the rook on f8, and the d7-knight belongs on c5, so securing it from being kicked with b4 later down the road was very important. However, I became very worried that I would get mated if White kept the bishop on h6, castles kingside and just starts amassing his forces to attack my king directly.

ANALYSIS DIAGRAM

Looking at it now with the engine's help, I think both parts are kind of true: the position is extremely dangerous, but only if White plays very precisely: 18.♗e2 ♘c5 19.♕g3!? (19.♕f3 ♘bd7 20.♕g2 ♕d8 21.0-0 ♕b6 does give Black legitimate counter-chances, for example) 19...♘bd7 20.0-0, and the idea of sending the queen to h4, and perhaps g5 afterwards, is quite potent, meaning that White can just ignore the fact the e4-pawn is hanging.

17.♗f4!?

I'm pretty sure Boris spent the sum total of three seconds on deciding not to play 17.♗h6 ♘e5 18.♗xf8 ♕xf8 19.♕xb7 ♘bd7, which suddenly gives Black full control over the dark squares, and plenty of counterplay.

17...♘f6?

I didn't like 17...♘e5 18.♗xe5 dxe5, since my knight is still too far away from the action and we've also closed down the best square we had for our knights. It's not a bad general assessment: after 19.fxg6 hxg6 20.g5, with the h4 and ♗h3 follow-up, Black is indeed in trouble. However, the text-move is worse.

18.♕f3?

The continuation of a series of mistakes, but we were both down to under 30 minutes on the clock, and had to navigate by feel in a very weird landscape – I know I have never seen anything like this structure before,

and I suspect that Boris hadn't either. Somehow neither of us realized how strong 18.e5! was: after 18...dxe5 19.♗xe5 ♘bd7 the bishop calmly returns: 20.♗f4, and Black is just stuck. The only source of 'counter-play' is 20...b5, but after the simple 21.0-0-0 it turns out to be ephemeral, and with ♖e1 and ♗d3 coming in, the position is about to collapse. In more general terms, I think it's completely decisive that Black no longer has access to the e5-square, and there are more files open than you will see in the game.

18...♘bd7

Now Black is well and truly back in the game

19.♗d3 b5?!

This looks pseudo-active, but in fact it was cleaner to establish a beach head on e5 before doing this.
19...♕c7 20.0-0 ♘e5 21.♕g3 ♘fd7 would have led to a fairly balanced position.

20.b3

My problem now is that I have to keep at least some brain cells occupied by the question 'is my b5-pawn hanging?', while taking on c4, when White can at least consider recapturing with the bishop, is potentially not that great either – I would like to have access to the b-file for later.

20...♖b8

I wasn't at all happy to spend a full tempo on this in a very concrete position, and having to hope that my indiscretion wouldn't be punished too severely.

21.0-0 ♘e5

"CAN I HAVE A MINUTE OF YOUR TIME? DO YOU THINK THERE IS SOMETHING AFTER THE ENDGAME?"

22.♕g3?
It's harsh to call this a mistake, but it was much more testing to play 22.♕e2!, and Black seems to be a tempo away from achieving the best set-up because it turns out that yes, b5 is hanging – and yes, we don't much like the prospect of ...bxc4 ♗xc4.
– 22...bxc4 23.♗xc4 ♘xc4 24.bxc4, and the threat of e4-e5, combined with the general weakness of my kingside, gives White a very serious edge.
– 22...♘fd7 runs into 23.cxb5!.
– And the naive 23...♘xd3 24.♕xd3 axb5 loses to 25.fxg6 hxg6 26.e5!.
– Perhaps the best choice is 22...♕d7, but after 23.♖ac1, introducing the additional threat of ♗xe5, cxb5 and ♖xc5, Black will struggle to coordinate his pieces properly.

22...bxc4?!
Starting with 22...♘fd7 was much cleaner, but we both thought the text-move would force 23.bxc4.

23.bxc4?! It's hard to criticize Boris for not realizing how strong 23.♗xc4! ♘xe4 24.♕g2! ♘xc4 25.bxc4 ♘f6 26.♗h6 ♖f7 27.♕e2 was. I don't think it's very obvious at all, even when I'm staring at the comp evalu-

ation telling me the game is basically lost. The 'simple' problem is – White will play ♕e6, and there will be no good way to react to it.

23...♘fd7

Now Black is doing completely fine for the first time in the game. The b-file is open, meaning White has to pay at least some attention to the queenside, while creating an attack on the other side of the board is difficult with the ♘d7-♘e5 tandem providing ample cover.

24.♗g5 We were both very short on time at this point, and this is a very understandable move, trying to create immediate questions that have to be answered.
The engine's suggestion 24.♗e2 ♖b2 25.♖ae1, completely abandoning the queenside and intending to play g5 and then try to get that bishop to g4, by hook or by crook, is a hard thing to even consider in time-trouble.

24...♖f7?! This is a good move, but played with a very panicky wrong idea. I left myself less than five minutes here, and finally decided on a course of action which gave White a draw if he wanted it, or a mess if he

didn't. The engine completely disagrees with this generosity and says 'you're already better, be thriftier'.
After 24...♖d8! White has no logical ways to continue to press on the kingside, and has to switch to defence.
25.fxg6 hxg6 26.♖xf7

26...♔xf7? 26...♘xf7! 27.♗xe7 ♕c7! gives Black a massive edge, because even with White to move, the impending ♘f7 plus ♘e5 set-up covers absolutely everything, e.g. 28.♖f1 ♘de5 29.♗f6 ♕a5!, and despite the very scary-looking bishop

'A good move, but played with a very panicky wrong idea'

on f6, there is just no attack, while the threat of ...♕c3 basically decides the game. I don't believe I spent more than 10 seconds on any of that, though.
27.♖f1+ ♔e8

28.♗c2!
This doesn't change the evaluation, but full marks to Boris for realizing

just how scary the thought of putting this bishop on a4 is.

I assumed his choices were a draw after 28.♗xe7 ♖xe7 29.♕h4+ ♔e8, completely missing that even here White can try 30.♗c2!, which would have forced me to find 30...♕c7! 31.♗a4 ♕a5, and shockingly, even with the bishop on a4, White still can't deliver mate versus those two majestic knights.

Or after the more ambitious and also weaker: 28.♕h4?! ♘d8 29.♗xe7+ ♔c7, when, despite being a pawn down, I was pretty sure I was in control, now that my king was safe.

28...♔d8!

With maybe two minutes left on the clock, this is the best move.

29.♗xe7+ ♔c7

29...♖xe7 30.♕h4+ ♔e8 31.♗a4 is completely lost: 31...♕b7 32.♕f6.

30.♗a4

Creating the threat of 31.♗xd6+! ♔xd6 32.♗xd7 and 33.♖f6+.

30...♕e8 It turns out it was possible to completely ignore the threat with 30...♖b4!?, though: 31.♗xd6+ ♔xd6 32.♗xd7 ♕b8!!, and the ideas of ...♔xd7 or ...♖b1 give Black enough play for the pawn. However, I don't think it's realistic to find this when moves like 30...♕e8, which give up precisely none of our remaining structure, exist.

31.♗f6

31.♗g5 ♘xc4 32.♗xd7 ♕xd7 33.♗f4 is also very far from clear, with the black king not nearly as safe on c7 as I thought during the game – but the text-move doesn't do any harm yet.

31...♖b4

32.♗xe5??

But this one does. Boris was down to seconds, which is the only way to explain him making such an unappealing move.

It took us a while during the postmortem to convince ourselves that after 32.♗xd7 ♘xd7 33.♕d3 Black has no way to collect any of the white pawns in the centre without allowing massive counterplay, but we finally decided it must be true, and the engine confirms that Black isn't even slightly better here, since trying to gang up on the c4-pawn will inevitably result in allowing e4-e5, often with disastrous consequences. The easiest way to ensure Black isn't worse either is to play 33...♖b2 34.♕a3 ♖b6, and the queen will have to go back to protecting e4: 35.♕d3 ♖b2 36.♕a3 ♖b6, with a draw.

32...♕xe5

Now White is simply lost.

33.♕a3 Or 33.♕xe5 ♘xe5 34.♗b3 a5, and everything crumbles.

33...d3 The cleanest.

34.♗xd7 ♖b2! 35.♕a5+ ♔xd7

White resigned.

■ ■ ■

For Jorden van Foreest and Boris Gelfand the tournament had started dramatically, with two losses each. In the third round they were paired against each other. Jorden will take us through that encounter, which catapulted him back into business.

NOTES BY
Jorden van Foreest

Jorden van Foreest
Boris Gelfand
Malmö TePe Sigeman 2023 (3)
Sicilian Defence, Accelerated Dragon

Both Boris Gelfand and myself had had a terrible start to the tournament, losing our first two games. Nevertheless, I was still looking forward to my first classical game against my legendary opponent, who was among the world's leading players even before I was born.

1.e4 c5 2.♘f3 ♘c6

Unsurprisingly, Gelfand remains steadfast in his strategy. Since his 2012 world championship match with Vishy Anand, he's been implementing this system, which has yielded him positive results.

3.♘c3

This is one of the ways to avoid the Sveshnikov, which often arises after 3.d4. The Rossolimo with 3.♗b5 is also very popular, and might be White's best chance for an objective advantage.

3...g6

Given that White can no longer

establish a Maroczy Bind, Black has the flexibility to transition into a more favourable variation of the Accelerated Dragon.

4.d4 cxd4 5.♘xd4 ♗g7 6.♗e3 ♘f6 7.♗c4 0-0 8.♗b3

All the standard moves have been completed, and now Black has a choice. I was not entirely sure what to expect, as Gelfand has tried virtually every move under the sun here.

8...d5

No, this is not a mouse-slip. It is actually one of the most direct attempts at equalizing the game, as the play now takes on a very forcing nature. In some more recent games, Gelfand had experimented with 8... a5, which leads to slower play.

9.exd5 ♘a5

In an ideal scenario, Black will capture on b3, reclaiming the d5-pawn with a comfortable position. However, reality is far more complex, and White will attempt to maintain control over the d5-pawn.

10.♕f3 ♘xb3 11.axb3 ♗g4 12.♕g3 ♗h5

The white queen has been drawn away from defending the d-pawn, but

the black bishop has ended up on the awkward h5-square, where it may be trapped at some point.

13.d6 Since the d-pawn has become a lost cause, White tries to surrender it under favourable circumstances.

13...♘g4

Black must play dynamically. In case of 13...exd6 14.0-0, White is structurally better and the bishop on h5 is also entirely out of the game.

14.h3 ♘xe3 15.fxe3 a6!

Gelfand played his subtlety quickly, clearly was still following his preparation. The idea is that instead of capturing on d6, Black actually wants to play ...e5, which would now be met by the unpleasant ♘db5.

16.♕h4 e5 17.♕xd8 ♖axd8 18.♘e6!

With this nifty little tactic, White finesses his way into an endgame that's just a touch more comfortable.

18...fxe6 19.g4 ♖f3

19...♖xd6 is also possible, but it would lead to a similar endgame after 20.♘e4, followed by an eventual 21.gxh5. With the text, Gelfand simplifies the position as much as possible.

20.♔e2 ♖xh3 21.gxh5 ♖xh1 22.♖xh1 ♖xd6

We're already 22 moves in, an endgame is on the horizon, and both of us are still following our preparation. There's some method to this madness, as we've both been playing the top engine line since move 8...d5. These days, you'll often spot players ditching a bit of objectivity just to spring a surprise on their opponents, but in this case, I was holding onto the hope that even if Gelfand knew all the moves leading up to the endgame, I could still try my chances at a win with the classic 'good knight versus bad bishop' scenario.

23.h6 On the morning of the game, I'd only given this position a quick glance, noting that both this move and hxg6 were deemed roughly equal by the engine.

The chosen move is a bit more decisive, as a significant part of the game will now hinge on whether the h6-pawn becomes an asset or a liability. It's not hard to imagine a scenario in which the h6-pawn is captured, leaving Black with two connected passers on the kingside.

That said, as long as the h6-pawn remains on the board, it serves to limit Black's mobility, particularly in terms of the black king's movements.

23...♗f8 24.♘e4 ♖c6 25.c3 ♗e7 26.♖f1

Jorden van Foreest had a dramatic start, but hit back with a win against Boris Gelfand.

It is crucial not to allow Black to play ...♔f7-e8, and to leave his king inside

the box that has been created on the kingside instead.

It was more or less this position that I was aiming for. Although the engine will show 0.00's, White's position remains easier to play. The fact that Black is up a pawn, is hardly felt, and White has a tremendous knight on e4. Moreover, even the pure rook endgames could start looking dicey for Black, with his king stuck on g8, completely cut off from the rest of the action.

26...♖c8

I spent some time considering 26...a5, with the idea of Black stopping b4, until I noticed a sweet idea for White: 27.♖a1 b6? (the ultra-passive 27...♖a6 is the only way to stay in the game) 28.b4! (forcing entry into the enemy camp) 28...axb4 29.♖a8+ ♔f7 30.♖h8, and White is winning.

27.b4

27...♖f8

The correct decision. Black needs to drive the white rook away from the f-file. Actually, the play takes on a very concrete nature now.

If Black simply stood and waited with 27...♖c6, he could quickly face serious trouble: 28.♔d3 ♖c8 29.♘f6+! (the key idea; by exchanging knight for bishop, the white king gains access to the e4-square) 29...♗xf6 30.♖xf6, with a super-dangerous rook ending for Black.

28.♖d1 ♖d8

Forced, as ♖d7 cannot be allowed.

29.♖xd8+ ♗xd8 30.♘c5

With the rooks now off the board, Black is presented with another headache: the queenside pawns are

> 'I was hoping I could still try my chances at a win with the classic "good knight versus bad bishop" scenario'

dropping like flies. All in all, this is shaping up to be a pretty dangerous situation for Black. When I got back to my hotel room after the game, I was surprised to discover that I had actually written down this exact position in my notes! Nowadays, most players tend to have everything written down in their files; the real challenge lies in being able to recall all that analysis when it matters.

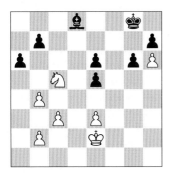

30...♗e7?!
The first really dubious decision in the game, which I frankly don't quite understand.
30...b6 was the move that I was expecting, and it is also the best move. At least in this way Black ensures that White does not get three passed pawns on the queenside all that easily.
31.♘xb7 ♔f7
Already a losing mistake – which goes to show how difficult the black position is to play. Only 31...e4 would have kept Black in the drawing zone, not allowing the white king to infiltrate along the light squares.
32.♔f3

32...g5
Another move that surprised me,

as I was expecting 32...♔e8. After 32...♔e8 33.♔e4 ♗f8 34.♘c5 ♗xh6 35.♘xa6 it turns out, however, that White's three passed pawns are stronger than Black's kingside pair.
33.♘c5?!
I was spending a lot of time around this time because everything was looking so good and I wanted to find the best continuation. As so often happens, all I managed to do was confuse myself in a web of variations. According to Stockfish, 33.♔g4 ♔g6 34.c4 was the cleanest way to win. I had seen the idea of giving up the b4-pawn in order to run with the c-pawn, but I thought Black's king would return in time: 34...♗xb4 35.c5 ♔f6.

ANALYSIS DIAGRAM

Here I only looked at 36.c6, which in fact is also winning, but I missed a very pretty solution to the problem: 36.♘d6!. This wins the game on the spot, as the white knight returns to the tremendous e4-square, from where it can collect the g5- and h7-pawns. 36...♔e7 37.♘e4.
33...a5

34.♘d3?

A mistake that objectively throws away the win! My idea was to keep two connected passers, but I should have played for domination instead: 34.c4! axb4 35.♘e4! (I must confess that I had not really considered this idea, and was focused on keeping my pawns alive instead. The idea is truly beautiful, as White not only keeps a few pawns alive, but also retain full domination) 35...♗f8 (the best defence) 36.♔g4 (White can even afford to lose the h6-pawn) 36...♗xh6 37.h5 ♗g7 38.♘xg5+ ♔e7 39.b3! (the key move, placing the pawn on a light square and not

> ## 'Even this is by no means entirely clear, but the Stockfish evaluation of +14 can be trusted'

allowing Black any more trades) 39...h6 (against other moves, White wins in a slow way, by pushing e3-e4, bringing the knight around to d3 and finally playing c4-c5 under the right circumstances) 40.♘e4 ♔f7

ANALYSIS DIAGRAM

41.c5!. The c-pawn acts as a decoy, which will ultimately allow the white king in. The variations remain complicated, but in the end there is no saving this for Black. A sample line continues as follows: 41...♗f8 42.c6 ♔e8 43.♔g6 ♗e7 44.♔xh6 ♔d8 45.♔g6 ♔c7 46.♔f7 ♗d8

The opening ceremony took place in the splendid Malmö Town Hall. While Gelfand adjusts his watch, youngsters Keymer, Gukesh and Erigaisi have a lot to talk about.

37...♗f8 37...g4 is a neat idea, but the g-pawn can be stopped just in time: 38.♘xh6 g3 39.♘d3! g2 40.♘xe5+ ♔f6 41.♘f3 ♔f5 42.♘h4+!. After some jumping around, the white knight manages to capture all Black's pawns.

37...♔g7 38.e4 is a nice zugzwang.

38.♔xg5 Here I felt I should be close to winning, as Black no longer has any counterplay on the kingside, and my two connected pawns will slowly but surely move down the board. Moreover, my knight has a beautiful square on d3, from where it controls both sides of the board and keeps the black king out of the game.

38...e4 Black's best chance; but it is already too late.

39.♔f4 ♗d6+ 40.♔xe4 h5 41.♘d3 h4

42.♘f4

Stopping the h-pawn in its tracks. 42.♔f3 h3 43.♘f4? was my initial intention, simply going after the h-pawn, but fortunately I noticed in time that this would give away the win: 43...h2 44.♔g2 ♔f6 45.♔xh2 ♔f5 (suddenly Black's king has become hyper-active, and White has lost coordination) 46.♔g2 ♔e4 47.♔f2 e5 followed by ♔d3, with enough counterplay for a draw.

42...♔f6

42...e5 is an ugly move, but it may have been the last chance of complicating things for White: 43.♘h3 ♔e6. The point is that for the moment it is not so easy for White to make progress. Indeed, after the rushed 44.b4 ♗e7 the position would no longer be winning. However, the

47.♔xe6 ♔xc6 48.♘d2!. Even this is by no means entirely clear, but the Stockfish evaluation of +14 can be trusted.

34...axb4 35.♘xb4

Perhaps 35.cxb4 would have been a better try, but I was very focused on keeping my two connected passed pawns. Regardless, at this point the game could be saved with optimal play from Black.

35...♗f8?

Gelfand immediately returns the favour. During the game I actually thought this was a good move, but it turns out to be the decisive error.

Correct was 35...e4+!. Before

embarking on the plan featured in the game, it was crucial to throw in this intermediate check. In general, the e5-pawn is only detrimental to Black's position, and giving it up gives the black bishop a lot more scope: 36.♔xe4 (36.♔g4 ♔g6! 37.♘c6 ♗c5 also saves the day for Black) 36...♗f8. White's king is far from ideally placed on e4, and after picking up the h6-pawn Black has enough counterplay.

36.♔g4!

This is the difference: now the white king enters on the kingside and Black loses one of his passed pawns.

36...♗xh6 37.♔h5!

slow plan of b3-c4-♘f2-♔f3-e4 is very effective and will win the game in the end.

43.♔f3

By this time, there is simply nothing Black can do, and White starts pushing the pawns on the queenside.

43...♔f5 44.b4 ♗e7 45.b5 ♗d8 46.c4 ♔e5 47.c5

Black resigned.

An important win for me, which brought me back into contention, and in the end I finished on a reasonable 3½/7.

■ ■ ■

For Boris Gelfand this amounted to a disastrous 0/3 start, but he showed admirable fortitude. Boris remained calm and collected, and after drawing Rounds 4 to 6, he still had a huge impact on the tournament in the final round.

That final round saw four people still in contention. Svidler and Mishra were sharing the lead, followed by Gukesh and Grandelius with half a point less. Despite provocations by his opponent, Jorden van

Foreest, who decided to meet 1.e4 e5 2.♘f3 ♘c6 3.♗b5 with the rarely played 3...f5, Nils decided to keep things clear and kept playing solidly. Their draw left only three players vying for first place. Svidler seemed to become a contender early on, as he had treated the early middle game impeccably. We join the game on move 27.

Gukesh D
Peter Svidler
Malmö TePe Sigeman 2023 (7)

position after 26...♗f8

A remarkable position. Black's queenside is locked up, yet the pieces locking it up are also themselves in danger. Moves like ...♔e7/♗e7 are looming, which makes White's next move all the more remarkable.

27.g3 Simply defending the f-pawn. It took a while before the penny dropped. 27...♔e7 28.♖d2! indirectly defends the knight on e8 and there is no other obvious way to continue. After some pondering, Peter continued with **27...♗e7**, before meeting

28.♘d6+ ♗xd6 29.♖xd6 ♗e6 30.b3 b5 31.♗e2 with the surprising **31...b4**

Now, with the queenside closed, White is out of the woods, and time-trouble started making itself felt.

32.♕d1 ♖e8 33.♗f3 ♗c8 34.♖xc6 ♕c3 35.♖c7+ ♔g8 36.♗e2 ♕e3 37.♕d5+ ♗e6 38.♕d3 ♕g1+ 39.♗d1 ♗f7 40.♕d7 ♖e7! A very nice 40th move to play. White is already on the right side of things now, and 40...♖f8 41.♕d2 would have left Black's queenside severely weakened. Svidler's move sets up a perpetual check if White captures the rook.

41.♖c8+?! Resigning himself to a draw. 41.♕d8+ was certainly worth a shot, when 41...♖e8 42.♕d2 is forced. Black is still fine here, with either 42...♕e4!? (43.♕d6 h5!) or even a slow move like 42...a5, but the game would have continued.

41...♔g7 42.♕xe7

And a draw was agreed.

This meant that all eyes were now on Mishra. Would he be able to make at least a draw and tie for first place? In the diagram below, the young

American had already done very well to get this far. Excellent opening play by Gelfand had led to a large advantage, but Mishra found some tough defensive moves and reached this soon-to-be queen ending.

Abhimanyu Mishra
Boris Gelfand
Malmö TePe Sigeman 2023 (7)

position after 44.f6

As I was explaining in the commentary room that 44...gxf6 was now the only move, since 44...h2 45.f7 h1♕ 46.f8♕ would leave White's strong e-pawn on the board, I was immediately put back in my place!
44...h2!? Objectively no better than 44...gxf6, but here 45.exf6 h2 46.f7 h1♕ 47.f8♕ should be a relatively easy draw against Black's a-pawn. Gelfand sets an interesting trap.
45.f7 h1♕ 46.f8♕ ♕h3+

This is the point! Without it, the previous sequence wouldn't make much sense. White is faced with some practical issues, since the king doesn't have an obvious square.
The natural 47.♔d5 will be met by 47...♕d3+ 48.♔e6 ♕c4+, which looks

scary, as the king can't go to d6 or e7. The engine points out 49.♔d7!, but this is easy to miss.
47.♔e7! is also good, but Mishra opts to swap the queens immediately.
47.♕f5+ Despite the fact that the engine barely considers this to be a mistake, I don't think I exaggerate when I say that this move eventually cost White the game. We now reach a queen ending in which Black has an extra g-pawn. Such pawns are notoriously hard to defend, however, especially with so little time on the clock.
47...♕xf5+ 48.♔xf5 a5

49.♔e6 White must waste this tempo, because 49.e6 ♔g8! would lose the spot.
49...a4 50.♔d6 a3 51.e6 a2 52.e7 a1♕ 53.e8♕ ♕d4+
A very nasty endgame, in which Black will slowly but surely advance his g-pawn. A full review of this endgame would be too much, but suffice it to say that it is incredibly hard to hold in a practical game. For the most part, Mishra did an admirable job, but he couldn't prevent Gelfand from eventually promoting the g-pawn some 70 moves later.

position after 122.♕d2

A telling picture of Abhi Mishra and Boris Gelfand after their game. The young American needed at least a draw for first place, but had to resign after 125 moves.

122...♕c6+! 123.♔b8 ♔h1
There are no checks left, and White can't pin the g-pawn either. That means it will inevitably queen on the next move. Mishra resigned shortly thereafter (0-1, 125).
And this is how Gelfand crowned his efforts with a much-desired victory. A real heartbreaker for Mishra, of course, but a mere 30 minutes afterwards, he was already seen playing blitz with the tournament winner!

And that means Peter Svidler, who, as always his modest self, expressed surprise at winning the event. Meanwhile, the rest of the world knows that winning eight Russian titles and an event like Malmö simply means that the person in question is a very strong chess player. So here's too him playing many more events in the future! ■

Margeir Petursson: 'There were days when I woke up and thought, what bad news will today bring?'

Margeir Petursson:

'Chess is quite a good preparation for a career in banking'

by DIRK JAN
TEN GEUZENDAM

Perhaps he should thank Bobby Fischer twice. Seeing the American win the world title in Reykjavik in 1972 ignited his love for chess. Seeing his childhood hero again 20 years later convinced him that his place was in the world of finance. Margeir Petursson's journey from professional grandmaster to prominent banker, first in Iceland and now in Ukraine, is an extraordinary success story. An interview with an accomplished player who never managed to forget his love for the Maroczy bind as his financial star kept rising.

'Yes, yes. I am no stranger to crises, you can say that.' Margeir Petursson laughs inaudibly at the understatement as we are talking about the turmoil and upheavals in his fascinating and successful second career. It's indeed an amusingly succinct and apt way of summarizing his life as a banker. In 2008, the former Icelandic chess champion first earned the attention – and admiration – of the international financial world when his bank managed to escape the near total collapse of the Icelandic banking system. Amid a shocking meltdown, Margeir Petursson's eponymous MP Bank was the only Icelandic bank that did not fail. He had refused to imitate the reckless risk-taking of his colleagues that had become the norm, had steadily sailed his own course, and was now rewarded for his common sense and caution. His bank also took a hit and lost 20% of its value, but it survived.

In his wish to explore new markets, his next big banking adventure took the Icelander to Ukraine. The promises and prospects were there and in 2006 he acquired Lviv Bank, now the biggest bank in western Ukraine. But it has been a stormy ride, with revolutions, international financial crises, Russian annexations of Ukrainian territory, Covid and finally the Russian invasion last year. 'There were days when I woke up,' he recalls, 'and thought, what bad news will today bring?'

His old chess friends in Iceland jokingly told him that he had been preparing for crises and suffering all his life. 'I like playing against the Maroczy bind, like Larsen and some others. But sometimes you get pushed back and

Margeir Petursson and company having dinner after a tournament at his chess club. On the left, Adrian Mikhalchishin, one of many grandmasters from Lviv. On the right, in the middle, Anna Muzychuk, another GM born in Lviv.

you have to defend a very difficult position. My friends were telling me to avoid such positions, but I very rarely lost. And they said, yes, that's your chess style and your business style – to defend a bad position.'

Lviv is at a pretty safe distance from the war that is mainly fought in the eastern part of Ukraine. Petursson (63) has been living there since 2011, after he sold his stake in his Icelandic bank (which allegedly made him one of the richest people in Iceland; something he denies: 'That's not true. I'm doing OK, but I am not at the top of the list, unfortunately'). When we talk in April, he says that everyday life has more or less returned to normal. 'We have the old traffic jams and parking problems again. There are no outages anymore and there's electricity all the time. Not the terrible problems we had in winter. Of course, people in general are very sad, and every day we have the army funerals. There are many people in the streets in military uniforms.'

But the desire to carry on and live life is strong. 'People are coming here for holidays from other parts of the country. There is a chess tourna-

ment coming up. A couple of weeks ago there was a huge simul in which many grandmasters took part.'

Petursson is a respected citizen

in Lviv, a city with some 700,000 inhabitants – not only because he is a prominent banker, but also because he is a chess grandmaster, a title that continues to be held in high esteem. For years he used to organize a monthly chess club in a room in the University Hotel. They played blitz and most of the participants were grandmasters. Now many chess players have left the country and the meetings have become considerably smaller. Only a handful take part and they gather in Petursson's office.

We speak on the phone. Although he is in Lviv and the connection is a bit creaky, the distance is not felt

as we had met in person and caught up only a week earlier when he was in The Hague for business. As we talk about chess, we return to his early beginnings. He wholeheartedly agrees that he was a child of the boom created by the Fischer-Spassky match in Reykjavik in 1972.

'That is absolutely right. I had been playing chess earlier, but I didn't fully understand that it was a much more serious game than other games. But before the match, I fully understood. The first time I visited an international tournament was in February 1972 [the match started in July – DJtG]. It was quite funny that the first grandmaster I saw playing in person was Leonid Stein, from Lviv. And now my office is in the same street as where he lived.

'I went to two games of the Fischer-Spassky match, and then I actually went to many adjourned games. Because people who went to the games could keep their tickets and I got them to see the adjournments

'The first grandmaster I saw playing in person was Leonid Stein, from Lviv, in 1972. And now my office is in the same street as where he lived'

for free. The tickets were quite expensive, 450 Icelandic Kroner, that's something like 25, 30 dollars today.

'Everything was possessed by the match that summer, so if you were a boy of 10, 12 or 16, and you didn't play chess, you were not taken seriously (laughs). Everybody played. That autumn there was a junior tournament, where I got second place and then, already in '73, I became Reykjavik Junior Champion. In 1975, I qualified for the Icelandic Championship final and finished shared first. That was only three years after the match, so that was very quick progress.'

Fruitful years followed, with two national championships, a victory in Hastings and successes with the 'golden Icelandic team' together with Johann Hjartarson, Helgi Olafsson and Jon Arnason. At the 1992 Manila Olympiad, they scored Iceland's best result ever by finishing in 6th place.

He regularly used to beat greats like Larsen (six times) and Portisch (twice) and also became an expert in open tournaments. 'I managed to be first in six quite strong open tournaments, in a period of less than a year. These tournaments are very difficult to win, but I managed to achieve that in a short period. Like the Lugano Open in 1989. I got 8 out of 9 and finished first with Korchnoi in a very strong field.'

In those years he fully dedicated himself to his chess career. 'In 1988, I had decided that I should either become a professional player or just give up chess. It was impossible to play with a certain consistency while at the same time having a difficult job. I was a lawyer for a state bank – I immediately went to work there when I finished my studies in '84 – and it was difficult to combine the two.'

Not an option

Petursson's years as a full-time chess professional were fairly successful – and certainly most enjoyable – but they ended sooner than he might have expected. Just like Bobby Fischer had drawn him into the magic of the game, the American also gave him compelling food for thought when he played his 'rematch' against Spassky in war-torn Yugoslavia twenty years later. 'That was a very important moment for me, when in '92 I went to the Sveti Stefan match as a chess correspondent for *Morgunbladid*. I was quite shocked when I saw my hero Bobby Fischer there and it somehow turned me away from devoting all my life to chess. After that it was not an option.'

Returning to the world of finance was the logical choice, and he believed that his experience as a chess player would be of help.

A few more banking details

When Margeir Petursson (who had 80% of the shares) and his partners sold the Icelandic MP Bank in 2011, the new owners were supposed to change the name of the bank. They only did so in 2015, leading one to believe that the initials were not so bad for business. In that year, the bank merged with Straumur Investment Bank and successfully continued as Kvika Bank. Initially, Petursson was the sole owner of Bank Lviv, which he acquired in 2006. In 2018, a Swiss private equity group took a 48% stake, and last January a Scandinavian fund acquired 14% of Bank Lviv. Petursson's stake now stands at around 38% (source: Euromoney.com).

Legends of Icelandic chess in 2014: Margeir Petursson, Helgi Olafsson, Fridrik Olafsson, Jon Arnason and Johann Hjartarson. All of them had just decided to take part in the 2015 European Teams in Reykjavik.

'Chess players are, at least I was, very analytical. We collect a lot of information and systemize it and then we have to make enlightened decisions. Chess is quite a good preparation for such a career. For many careers.

'Because of my chess training, I acquired, like most chess players, a quite independent mind, and I realized that I couldn't go back to the bank and be subordinate to someone at the office. So I had to start my own business. It was an investment business and it went OK. First I did it on the side, together with chess, and then I went into it totally fulltime. But it was extremely hard work. I even went back to university, I took courses, everything that could help my investment career.'

How did you get from having an investment company to owning a bank in Iceland?
'It went gradually. First I got a licence and I took on clients through investment management. Then I had people working for me and we were also brokers. That was the first license we got, as brokers and investment managers. And then we got the whole investment banking license in 2003. We grew quite rapidly and then, in 2008, we got the full banking license.'

In the dramatic year of the immense Icelandic banking crisis.
'Yes. The authorities actually gave us that license because all the other banks were basically broke and they wanted to have at least one sound bank operating. Because there were terrible, terrible problems in Iceland's banking relations. Everyone locked down on Iceland, but I still managed to keep my international banking relations open. And my colleagues in international banks appreciated that we could fulfil our obligations. It's a license that is extremely difficult to get, and all your competitors try to keep you out of the game. There

Margeir Petursson in front of Bank Lviv wearing a jacket he would not have worn before the Russian invasion of Ukraine.

was the clearing centre that the other banks owned and they just laughed when we tried to enter that system. But then, after the crisis, they could no longer refuse us.'

primitive market. It was difficult to do anything. With that experience I really wanted to participate in the Baltic countries, in the development of the financial systems. The Baltic countries entered the European Union in 2004, and there was a lot of money coming into these countries. My partners and I decided, let's just sell our investments there and go to a new market. We chose Ukraine and I was very optimistic because at the end of 2004 we had the Orange Revolution and we were optimistic about the new president, who had been the head of the national bank. It was an interesting step to take. Just by chance we found a very small bank in Lviv in 2005. There was infighting with shareholders and I saw an opportunity and managed to buy the bank relatively cheaply. But the optimism of 2004 was not justified and Ukraine got into huge trouble in the banking crisis in 2008 and 2009. So it's been no picnic, you can say that.

'When we started to develop Bank Lviv, I made the decision that we would not cross the Dnieper river. We would focus on the western part of the country. That turned out to

'I was quite shocked when I saw my hero Bobby Fischer in Sveti Stefan. It somehow turned me away from devoting all my life to chess'

While this adventure was unfolding, you had already started another adventure in Ukraine. How did that come about?
'I was already in the Baltic countries from 2003 and 2004, and in Ukraine from 2004. We were mostly in bonds and stock markets. We had investment banking licenses in many countries. I considered myself a kind of specialist in emerging and primitive markets. When I worked in a bank in the 1980s it was an extremely

be a very fortunate decision. The two parts are very different, and western Ukraine would never want to be part of Russia. The population is quite homogenous, they speak the Ukrainian language and they are more western orientated. We are very close to Europe.'

Do you speak both Russian and Ukrainian?
'I wish I could say that. I understand both languages in written form, but

I am a much more fluent Russian speaker. I have been working on my Ukrainian for the last two, three years. It's a difficult language for Westerners, but since I have been fluent in Russian for so many years, it's easier.

'In Soviet times the people here read more Russian than Ukrainian, but now it's completely different. People read Ukrainian on principle. In the bookshops here you don't have any Russian books.'

Did you learn Russian for the same reason that Fischer tried to get a grasp of the language? To read chess literature?
'Yes, that's how it was originally. And it turned out to be very practical for business in the early 2000s. I started Russian in the Gymnasium, I studied it for three years. It was my third language.'

Who are your favourite Russian authors?
'From my young years I have to say it was Chekhov. I read the complete short stories of Chekhov when I was 20 years old. Later I have become quite a fan of Dostoevsky.'

Did you foresee the Russian invasion? Did you think it was possible it might happen?
'I thought about it and people had been predicting it ever since 2014. This war basically started in 2014, when Russia tried to grab territories in Ukraine. The situation stabilized and it was rather stable till the end of 2021, when there were predictions of Russia invading from intelligence sources. I actually didn't believe that they would be foolish enough to attack. I was convinced they could never take the whole country and there would just be partisan fighting. If they managed to get to Kyiv, it would be just foolish to think they could keep those territories. That was my analysis.
'I explained to my friends and

colleagues that Russians are quite good chess players, most of them, and good chess players understand that often the threat is stronger than its execution. It forces one's opponent to make concessions. And that was what I thought the Russians were doing, but then they turned out to be absolute patzers. These things are not controlled by a great chess mind, that's clear.'

What are your expectations concerning the war?
'It's just very difficult to say. If there is a Ukrainian counter-attack in the next two, three months, and it looks like that's going to happen, then it's possible to predict something. And in such situations it's very important to think who has time on their side. The Russians probably think time is on their side, but I am not convinced.

Margeir Petursson together with grandmaster Oleg Romanishin on his 70th birthday in January 2022.

I think it could be on the Ukrainian side if this drags on.'

What has been the impact for your business?
'It has affected us surprisingly little. Before this there was Covid. Covid was difficult; we had to reschedule many loans. Now it's the war restructuring. We have excellent clientele and they want to honour their obligations and are quite resilient. So far we have not suffered that much. We were growing quite quickly, but that growth has almost stopped.'

You have been through so many upheavals and crises. How did you manage to keep your equilibrium?
'You have to expect things and try to figure out things beforehand, when you see the economic trends. For me, chess is very important, again. I hardly followed chess for almost 15 years, but lately I've come back. I had enough of chess. I wanted to focus on a new career, but I am enjoying it again. Since Covid I've been following all the main tournaments. I am very grateful to Magnus Carlsen for saving the sanity of chess players by organizing all these online events in the year 2020. He did a great job. After this I spent a lot of time on chess, following the new openings. I have many chess-playing friends in Ukraine and here everyone knows that I am a chess grandmaster.'

And you even played for the Icelandic national team again at the Chennai Olympiad.
'I have been captain of the Icelandic team twice now, at the European Team Championship in 2021 and last year in Chennai. Just before we left for India, we got the bad news that our youngest player, the newly crowned GM Vignir Vatnar Stefansson had been diagnosed with Covid and couldn't go. All our players had to play more games than if Vignir had been around, and even I had to step in as a reserve after a 26-year break

from the Olympics. Of course, I spent a lot of time criticizing the players for not playing practically, and spoiling games in time-trouble. Most of the time they ignored my reasonable demand that after 20 moves they should have half an hour left to reach the 40-move time-control. I vainly quoted GM Gudmundur Sigurjonsson, who told us youngsters in the 1970s: 'To lose a game due to time-trouble is no better excuse than that

'Gudmundur Sigurjonsson told us youngsters in the 1970s: "To lose a game due to time-trouble is no better excuse than that of the driver in an accident who says he was drunk"'

of the driver in an accident who says he was drunk.' Anyway, the players did well and I played three games. I made two draws and I won in the last round, contributing to our victory over Bulgaria, 2,5-1,5, so I was quite happy to end my Olympic career on that note. Icelandic chess is in terrible trouble if they have to recruit me again.'

After we concluded our talk, I asked Margeir Petursson to annotate his last Olympiad game. He agreed that it was an instructive win and soon sent me his annotations. However, when he did so, he must have felt that this game could hardly be seen as representative for his best chess years, so he asked me if he could present one of his more memorable games to our readers as well. That sounded like an excellent plan, and my initial idea was confirmed when the game arrived.

While in the first game the cautious, planning hand of the banker may be seen, his spectacular win against Djurhuus from 1995 is a demonstration of attacking zeal and combinational brilliance.

my young opponent had prepared against my usual Averbakh Variation. After my humble 3.g3 I could sense that he was a bit disappointed.

3...e5 4.♗g2 ♘e7 5.e3

5...0-0
Here or on the next move, Black could have disrupted my plans by playing ...c7-c6!?
6.♘ge2 c5
Giving up the d5-square by placing pawns on c5 and e5 seems less logical here than after White has already committed his knight to f3. But this has been played by strong GMs like the young Karpov, Kavalek and others.
7.a3 ♘bc6 8.d3 d6 9.0-0 ♗e6

NOTES BY
Margeir Petursson

Margeir Petursson
Todor Georgiev
Chennai Olympiad 2022
English Opening

1.c4 g6 2.♘c3 ♗g7 3.g3
I did not want to engage in a theoretical battle but to steer the game into a quiet flank opening. I suspected that

10.♘d5 ♖b8 11.♘ec3 a6

12.b4?!
More accurate was 12.♖b1 b5 13.b4, with the same position as in the game. Now Black could have played 12...e4!, with an unclear game.
12...b5 13.♖b1

13...bxc4
Accepting my pawn sacrifice, and with all the white pawns on the queenside eliminated, it looks as if Black is quite safe. But maintaining the tension with 13...♕d7 would have been better.
14.dxc4 cxb4 15.axb4 ♗xd5 16.cxd5 ♘xb4 17.♕a4 a5 18.♗d2

18...♕b6?!

Now White regains the pawn and keeps a strong bishop pair. Black, however, manages to exchange queens.

In case of 18...♕c7, White has pleasant compensation after 19.e4.

19.♘a2 ♕b5 20.♕xb5 ♖xb5 21.♘xb4 axb4 22.♖xb4

It is understandable that Black did not want to go for the joyless endgame against the bishop pair that would arise after 22...♖fb8 23.♖fb1 ♖xb4 24.♖xb4 ♖xb4 25.♗xb4. To start with, White will play e3-e4 and then bring his king over to the queenside, where the monarch will take up residence on b7 or b6. But Black has a rather small territory to defend, so this was his best chance. These days, however, there is less faith in fortresses than 30 to 40 years ago.

22...♖c5? 23.e4 ♖c2 24.♗e3

Now the bishop pair and the rook on an open file dominate.

24...f5 25.♖b7

25...f4?!

Hastening defeat.

26.♗c1! ♘c8 27.♗h3 h5 28.♗a3 ♖c3 29.♗b2 ♖c4 30.♖c1 ♖xc1+ 31.♗xc1 f3 32.♗g5

Black resigned.

We managed to defeat Bulgaria 2½-1½ in the ever important final round and finish higher than expected. After this low-energy game and always with plenty of time on the clock, I turned to my teammates and asked them: 'Why didn't you just play like me?' Anyway, a nice end to my long Olympic career, which started in 1976 and should have ended in 1996, when I played first board for Iceland.

NOTES BY
Margeir Petursson

Margeir Petursson
Rune Djurhuus
Gausdal International 1995
King's Indian Defence, Averbakh Variation

I loved playing in Gausdal, Norway, enjoying the mountain air. The late Arnold J. Eikrem, whom I regard as the godfather of the Norwegian chess boom, organized many tournaments there. In the following entertaining game I face a difficult opponent, Norwegian GM Rune Djurhuus, with whom I had a score to settle, because he had beaten me in the Moscow Olympiad in 1994, depriving me of a board prize. Apart from being a talented and original chess player, Rune is a very successful software engineer.

1.d4 ♘f6 2.c4 g6 3.♘c3 ♗g7 4.e4 d6 5.♗e2 0-0 6.♗g5

My favourite Averbakh Variation. These days, 6.♗e3, with many similar ideas, is more popular.

6.....♘a6 7.♕d2 e5 8.d5 ♕e8 9.♗d1

9...♘c5 Bologan gives 9... c6 in his repertoire book from 2017. In a new book on the Averbakh Variation authored by Jan Boekelman, the author shows that 9.....c6 is a more difficult move to meet than 9....♘c5.
10.♗c2 a5 11.♘ge2 ♗d7 12.f3 This position resembles the KID, Sämisch Variation, that starts with 5.f3. It is a favourable version for White.
12...h5

13.♗e3
I played an improvement over 13.h3 ♘h7 14.♗e3 h4 15.g4 in Petursson-Nunn, London Lloyds Bank 1994.

ANALYSIS DIAGRAM

Margeir Petursson takes on Garry Kasparov in a rapid tournament in Kopavogur in 2000. He lost to the World Champion but finished third behind Kasparov and Anand.

That game continued 15...♕e7 16.♖g1 f6?! 17.f4 ♗h6 18.0-0-0 a4 19.♕e1 g5? 20.f5, and White should be strategically winning, although I lost that game. Previously, I had managed to beat Nunn twice with the Averbakh. I was worried about the improvement 15...hxg3 16.♘xg3 f5, but now (2023) I realize, with the help of computers, that after 17.exf5 gxf5 18.♖g1! White is much better. White should actually play 15.g3! (instead of 15.g4) to aim for this line.
In the top game Grischuk-Radjabov, Biel 2007, White chose 13.0-0 – a very surprising decision by the first-board player of the Russian Communist Party Chess team. White should go for a kingside attack and hide his own king on the other side.
13...♘h7 14.0-0-0

14...b6 14...f5 would run into 15.exf5 gxf5 16.♗xc5 dxc5 17.d6 c6 18.♘a4.
15.h3 h4
15...f5?! would only speed up White's attack after 16.exf5 gxf5 17.g4!.
16.g3!

16...♕e7?! Quite slow, but after 16....f5 White is clearly better after both 17.♖dg1 or 17.exf5.
17.♖dg1 a4 18.f4 I thought this to be the logical continuation of the attack and gave it an exclamation mark in my notes. However, modern programs prefer 18.gxh4, followed by rook-doubling on the g-file. This seems a bit slow to me, however.
Now, after my move 18.f4, the computers recommend 18....exf4 19.gxf4 ♘f6 20.e5! dxe5 21.f5 ♘b3+!, when White will end up

being slightly better after 22.axb3 axb3 23.♗b1 ♖a1 24.fxg6 ♗f5 25.gxf7+ ♕xf7 26.♖xg7+! ♕xg7 27.♖g1 ♘g4! 28.hxg4 ♗xb1 29.♘xb1 ♕g6 30.♘c3 – one of those forced computer lines that look like science fiction to us humble humans.

18.....♔h8 19.gxh4

19.f5 was also good.

19...♕xh4?!

Now White's attack gains traction. 19....exf4 20.♘xf4 ♗e5 was preferable.

20.f5 gxf5 21.exf5

21...♖g8 After 21...♕xc4?, 22.♖g4 ♕a6 23.f6 is crushing.

22.♖g4 ♕e7 23.♗g5! ♗f6

23...♘xg5 24.♖h4+ ♘h7 25.f6, and White wins.

24.h4

'My satisfaction with this game was confirmed by it being voted the 4th best game of Chess Informant 64'

24...e4!

The only practical try for counterplay. Otherwise the manoeuvre ♘g3 to h5 or e4 would maintain full control.

25.♘xe4 ♘xe4 26.♖xe4 ♕f8 27.♘g3 a3 28.b3 ♗b2+ 29.♔b1 f6

Black wants to place his bishop on e5, which would halt White's attack.

30.♖e6

The most aesthetically pleasing move of my entire career.

30...♗e5 31.♘e4 ♗xe6

Black is paralysed, so he might as well grab material to show something for his suffering.

32.dxe6 c6 33.♗h6 ♕e7

34.♘g5!! fxg5 35.hxg5 ♖a7 36.♕d3

A good move, but 36.g6 would also have won.

36...♗f6

An attempt to break out by 36...♖xg5 37.♗xg5 ♕xg5 fails to 38.f6! ♔g8 39.f7+ ♔f8 40.♕xh7 ♕g7 41.♖xg7+ ♗xg7 42.♖g1, and the pawns on e6 and f7 decide.

37.gxf6 ♕xf6 38.♗c1 d5 39.cxd5 cxd5 40.♖h6 ♕e5 41.f6

Here the game was adjourned. Rune sealed **41...♖g1,** with the threat of 42...♕b2 mate, but resigned without further play, as 42.♖xh7+ ♔g8 43.f7+ ♔f8 44.♗d1! will lead to Black getting mated instead.

My first thought after winning this game was that I could now quit chess with full dignity after writing a book on the Averbakh System, which I did the following year. My satisfaction with this game was confirmed by it being voted the 4th best game of *Chess Informant* 64 by a grandmaster panel. ■

In Graphic Detail

A graphic novel biography of Bobby Fischer is an intriguing idea, but can a book primarily made up of drawings capture the complexity of Fischer's life?

by JOSEPH G. PONTEROTTO

Whatever doubts I may have had, I was pleasantly surprised by the joint effort of Julian Voloj and Wagner Willian. Their book, *Black and White, The Rise and Fall of Bobby Fischer*, is a graphically vivid, historically accurate, and psychologically informed contribution to both chess history and the broader area of psychohistory.

The story is told by Julian Voloj, a New York-based writer with a passion for chess, whose work includes graphic novels about the painter Basquiat and about Joe Shuster, the artist behind Superman. Wagner Willian is an award-winning comics and visual artist.

Their research was based on popular books on Fischer, such as Frank Brady's *Endgame*, Edmonds and Eidinow's *Bobby Fischer Goes to War*, as well as Olafsson's *Bobby Fischer Comes Home* as a source on his final years in Iceland. They also cite the Liz Garbus HBO documentary, *Bobby Fischer against the World*.

The physical features of the book are impressive: a sturdy, hardcover volume with 170 thickly textured pages consisting of (by my count) 920 black and white images of various shapes and sizes. The book is organized along eight chapters that trace Fischer's life chronologically and developmentally, from his first introduction to the game when his older sister

Joan bought him a plastic chess set at the local candy/toy store, to his death in Reykjavik.

The story traces Fischer's introduction to local competition and meeting his first chess teacher/mentor, Carmine Nigro. Fischer's commitment to all things chess, to the exclusion of other important life activities, is presented in a sequence of images that include a young Fischer with his library chess books, and his studying chess with sandwich in hand and in the bathtub. Regina Fischer's concern over her son Bobby's sole focus on chess is captured, as is her bringing him to a psychiatrist for an assessment.

Roughly midway in the book, Fischer is introduced to the Marshall Chess Club. He starts to show his deep talent for chess, and he travels to his first significant tournament, the U.S. Junior Nationals in Lincoln, Nebraska. Pivotal at this stage for his personal and professional development was being introduced to mentor and teacher Jack Collins and his wife Ethel, who lived not too far from Fischer's high school, Erasmus, in Brooklyn, NY. With Regina Fischer working lengthy hours, the Collins' residence became like a second home for young Fischer.

At this point in the story, Fischer's gift for chess is apparent to all. A historic moment captured over two full pages is his win over IM Donald Byrne in the 'Game of the Century'. The authors then delve into the FBI's surveillance of Regina Fischer for her communist sympathies and the stress it causes the whole family. Fischer's appearance as a contestant on the "I've got a Secret" T.V. game show is presented, where we also see the supportive role of his older sister Joan, who then served as his chaperone on his first trip to the Soviet Union.

Understandably, a strong emphasis in the book is the 1972 championship match in Reykjavik. A series of images highlight the famous Henry Kissinger call to an ambivalent Fischer to encourage him to go ahead with the match against Spassky, Fischer's litany of complaints surrounding the match playing conditions, and the Spassky team's insistence that Fischer's chair be deconstructed in a search for electric devices. And there's the pivotal back-room Game 3, Fischer's first win, and an inflection point for the match.

The later parts of the book take the reader to Los Angeles post-match, where Fischer grew increasingly isolated after leaving his supporters at the Worldwide Church of

God. Vivid images capture Fischer's growing anti-Semitism and increasing paranoia. Scenes of his brief stay with his sister Joan's family in Palo Alto, depict the family asking him to leave because of his anti-Semitism.

When 17-year-old Zita Rajcsanyi visits Fischer in L.A., his wilderness years come to an end as he agrees to a rematch with Spassky. Scenes then shift to Yugoslavia and the 1992 match

white-bearded Fischer sprawled on his death bed surrounded by images representing memories from the past, followed by final scenes of Fischer's burial in Selfoss, Iceland.

While this biography is generally very accurate historically, the authors do take some dramatic license in emphasizing select scenes. For example, a few images during Fischer's 'wilderness' years depict

and life. In the first case in L.A., his increasing paranoia; and in the 1956 Manhattan Chess Club scene, his impressive victory over Byrne.

The scope of coverage is wide, though there are two scenes (relationships) that I would like to have seen covered. One scene could depict Fischer's 'search' for his father, with images of his almost look-alike probable father, Dr. Paul Nemenyi, and with Fischer looking up, wondering about his father. It would also behoove the Fischer story to have an image of Fischer with GM William Lombardy in Reykjavik, 1972, given his crucial role in helping Fischer analyze adjourned games and convincing him to stay when Fischer was about to abort the match after Game 2. ∎

'While this biography is generally accurate historically, the authors do take some dramatic license'

Joseph G. Ponterotto is a psychologist and the author of A Psychobiography of Bobby Fischer: Understanding the Genius, Mystery and Psychological Decline of a World Chess Champion (2012, Charles C Thomas, Publisher). He is currently a tenured professor of counseling psychology and the Coordinator of the School Counseling Program at Fordham University's Graduate School of Education.

in Sveti Stefan and Belgrade. Particularly striking is Fischer defying the U.S. Treasury Department order not to play the match, and his reaction by spitting on the document at a press conference.

Voloj and Willian present a few images of the 9-11 terrorist attacks and of Fischer expressing his joy in the attacks on a radio broadcast. The closing sections of the graphic biography cover Fischer's 2004 arrest at Tokyo's Narita Airport, followed by his release and resettlement in Reykjavik for his remaining years. Several scenes portray Reykjavik as a cold and snowy city where Fischer grows increasingly isolated as his unshakeable anti-Semitism eventually distances his former Icelandic friends and allies. The book's closing graphics depict a

him driving a car and looking behind him and to his side, as if suspicious that he is being followed. In my research on Fischer during that period, I do not remember any evidence of him driving a car in L.A. (or elsewhere).

Another dramatic liberty is seen earlier in the 'Game of the Century' with Donald Byrne, where their chess table is being crowded by spectators and one onlooker exclaims 'Impossible, Byrne is losing to a 13-year-old nobody'. The scene most likely did not unfold this way given the Manhattan chess club etiquette. However, taking dramatic license is rare in the biography, and when incorporated, serves to highlight critical 'moments' in Fischer's career

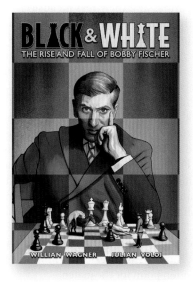

Black & White: The Rise and Fall of Bobby Fischer, Julian Voloj and Wagner Willian, 176 pp, Abrams ComicArts, New York, 2023.

Allan Rufus: 'Life is like a game of chess. To win you have to make a move. Knowing which move to make comes with insight and knowledge, and by learning the lessons that are accumulated along the way. We become each and every piece within the game called life.' *(The American author and Corporate and Life Coach, in his motivational book The Master's Sacred Knowledge)*

Perpetual Ogbiyoyo: 'Chess is not just a sport to me. It is like my escape.' *(The Nigerian two-time women's chess champion)*

Vladimir Tukmakov: 'Soviet professional chess was a school of survival.'

Oscar Panno: '[Chess is] a bloodless war in which the soldiers go to the box and not to the cemetery. If you read *The Art of War* by Chinese author Sun Tzu, you will realise that a lot of the advice and observations are valid for chess. And vice versa: the concepts are applicable to war situations.' *(The Argentinian grandmaster, who celebrated the 70th anniversary of becoming the 2nd World Junior Champion with a tournament in his honour, running 9-16 May, in Villa Martelli)*

Alireza Firouzja: 'I wanted to always have something outside of chess because just to play chess your whole life is a bit weird for me. I always loved playing chess, but the fact that I'm living in Paris now... there's a good opportu-nity there.' *(Speaking during the Superbet Chess Classic Romania on his decision to seek a career in fashion)*

Forest Whitaker: 'I love to play chess. The last time I was playing, I started to really see the board. I don't mean just seeing a few moves ahead – something else. My game started getting better. It's the patterns. The patterns are universal.' *(The chess-loving Hollywood actor also likes to strategically place chess sets — or even chess pieces — in the background of his film scenes)*

Fabiano Caruana: 'That's the thing about chess: If you don't have any familiarity with it, it just means nothing to you.'

GM Joe Gallagher: 'One of the greatest advantages of chess over other sports is that you can always resign.'

Robert Sapolsky: 'When you look at these chess Grand Masters who've just taken down an opponent, they will have the exact same physiology of some wild baboon in the savannah who has just ripped open the stomach of his worst rival.' *(The eminent professor of neurology and neurosurgery at Stanford University, on his study on the stress of playing chess)*

Bent Larsen: 'All chess masters have on occasion played a magnificent game and then lost it by a stupid mistake, perhaps in time pressure and it may perhaps seem unjust that all their beautiful ideas get no other recognition than a zero on the tournament table.'

Max Euwe: 'Alekhine can see five or six times as much as I can, but I have a plan, and that plan sometimes permits me to win.' *(Said on the eve of his successful 1935 World Championship match)*

Bobby Fischer: 'That man is too normal. There must be something wrong with him.' *(After meeting Max Euwe for the first time)*

Boris Spassky: 'I came to know [Tigran] Petrosian very well. He was just an open book for me. He was a hot-tempered man. When he was walking quietly I knew that he was about to jump like a panther; on the contrary, when he was moving like Napoleon it was always a sign of cowardice.'

Mikhail Botvinnik: 'The world champions die in the strict order of their succession to the title. Thus the writer of these lines is the next on the list. I telephoned Smyslov and reminded him that after me it would be his turn. Smyslov laughed; indeed, as long as I am alive he can afford to laugh!' *(After Max Euwe's death in 1981. The following year, Tigran Petrosian died, the first world champion out of sequence)*

The Worst Move on the Board

We've been told countless times to look for the best move in the position in front of us. But what about the worst move on the board? The WMOTB?
It can make a lot of sense to spot that one too!

by JUSTIN HORTON

You've probably seen this position. It's Giri-Rapport, final round at Wijk aan Zee 2023. White has just played the knight from f4 to h5 with check.

So you'll probably already know that Black played **34...♔g6**, a move which lost by force to 35.♖xd6, which won, after 35...♔g5 36.♖d5 ♕e1+ 37.♔g2 ♗e7 38.♖xf5+ ♔h4 39.♕g3+, both the game and the tournament. What you might not have realised is that of the five legal moves available to Rapport, the one he selected was the only one which loses.

The other four are fine: only Rapport's choice loses material. Hence the move that Rapport played was The Worst Move On The Board.

What's the Worst Move On The Board? We'll sort out some definitions later, but they're something I began to notice a few years ago, after I happened idly to be looking at the game Short-Beliavsky from Linares 1992. Can you see what White played?

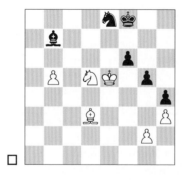

Nigel finessed with **58.♔e6**, which move lost immediately. As immediately as can be, because Black played 58...♗c8 mate. It's not the only move that loses, since 58.♔f5 drops the

knight, but losing a piece is no match for an instant loss. In fact there's no other way to allow a mate in one. So 58.♔e6 is the Worst Move On The Board (or WMOTB, for short).

That's pretty funny, I thought, and once I started looking for them, other examples started cropping up. For instance I was looking at Willy Hendriks' *Move First, Think Later* where, in the introduction, he gives the following position, from Dam-Hendriks, Dutch Youth Championship 1985, with Black to play.

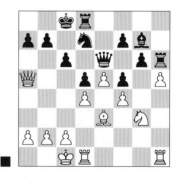

In contrast with our previous examples, where the king was in check, Black has thirty moves available. He even has three ways of putting his queen *en prise* to a pawn. But why lose your queen when you can lose the game immediately? There's a WMOTB to be played and Hendriks found it, playing **20...♚b8** which was met by 21.♕xd8 mate.

This next one popped up on my Twitter timeline just a few months ago. It's from a game Praggnanandhaa-Duda in the FTX Crypto Cup 2022, and it's Pragg to move.

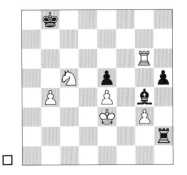

The sponsor, you'll recall, imploded in a spectacular manner shortly after the tournament took place. As indeed Pragg had done already, the WMOTB, **55.♘d3**, having allowed Duda to mate in one.

That's three consecutive mates in one, and yes, a WMOTB is often an instant mate. But here's a slightly longer finale, from Batuev-Simagin, USSR Team Championship, Riga 1954. Black has a lot of ways to lose quickly, and for that matter, a number of ways to win slowly. But what's the WMOTB? What's the fastest way for him to lose?

The Worst Move On The Board is the move which loses to the fastest mate, or is the only move that loses, or is the move which loses the most material, or is the only move that does not win

Simagin found **84...e2**, allowing mate in three with 85.♕g1+ ♚d2 86.♕c1+ ♚d3 87.♕c3 mate.

Hopefully by now you're trying to guess the WMOTB before reading further to see what was played. Have a go at this one from Atalik-Sulava, Tekirdag 2016. White to play.

Indian star Praggnanandhaa normally does better than allowing a mate in 1.

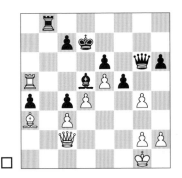

Atalik played **32.gxf5** which allows Black a mate in six with 32...♖b1+ 33.♗c1 (33.♔xb1 ♕xg2 mate) 33...♖xc1+ 34.♔f2 ♕xg2+ 35.♔e3 and Black has a choice of routes to a mate on move 37 e.g. 35...♕g1+ 36.♕f2 ♖e1+ 37.♔d2 ♕xf2 mate.

It's the WMOTB. But to be sure of that, you'll have had to analyse the alternatives! For instance, you might think that 32.♕b1

would succumb just as swiftly, but in fact after 32...♖xb1+ 33.♔f2 White can keep going until move 38, as after 33...f4 (33...♕xg4 lets White play e6+ and g3 and stave off mate a further move) there is 34.♖xd5+ exd5 and then White has e6+ and ♗c1 as spoilers.

So you have to do a bit of work, just as you would with a problem or a study. And the WMOTB is really a problem, a problem with its own specifications.

What are these? In the first place, that the WMOTB is the move which loses to the fastest mate. But that won't do for all occasions, because there isn't always a demonstrable mate.

It won't for instance do for Giri-Rapport. Nor for Chigorin-Schlechter, Ostend 1905, White to play.

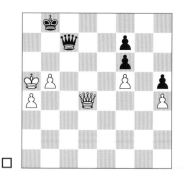

Chigorin played **45.♕b6+**, which allowed 45...♔a8 drawing by stalemate (46.♕xc7) or by repetition (46.♔a6 ♕c8+). There's no mate, but where Rapport found the only move that lost, Chigorin found the only move that didn't win – which is also the WMOTB.

It won't do for this position, from a 2019 internet game. White to play.

White has all manner of bad moves available (and not very many good ones) but **7.♗e2** is the only one to lose the queen (to 7...♘xe3). It's the WMOTB because, although no demonstrable end to the game is available, there's no other move which loses quite as much material.

So we can define our terms as follows. **The Worst Move On The Board is the move which loses to the fastest mate, or is the only move that loses, or is the move which loses the most material, or is the only move that does not win.**

Yes, a WMOTB is often an instant mate

We can add some riders. To be a proper WMOTB, it should really have been played in a game. It's maybe not compulsory, but what's a joke without its punchline? Also, there are *definitely* no joint WMOTBs in a position. If there are, there is no WMOTB. It's like a problem that is cooked.

Also, just because there's only one WMOTB in a position doesn't mean there's only one way for the opponent to prove it. Take this position, for instance, from Brown-Robinson, South Wales International 2012.

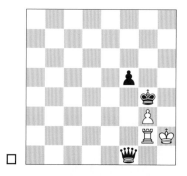

White to play is obviously already lost – just because you're losing doesn't mean you can't find a WMOTB – but not actually obliged to lose straightaway, which **1.♖g1** would have achieved had Black spotted the mate in one it permitted.

But 1...♕h3 mate isn't the only move to win – in fact there are eight other moves that preserve the win (and Black did, indeed, win in the end). It doesn't matter! There could be fifty winning replies to the WMOTB – but only one WMOTB, and that's the point.

How should we annotate the WMOTB? I've left them neutral up to now, but I confess I have a liking for marking them with the double exclamation mark that indicates the most exceptional moves. For what could be more exceptional than the Worst Move On The Board?

This is one of my favourites, from Arkell-Osborne, Sunningdale 2013, White to play.

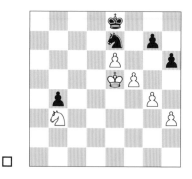

White found **42.♘a5!!** allowing Black to play 42...♘c6+ forking the king and knight *with his own knight*. A quite exceptional WMOTB, and if you find one more deserving of those two exclamation marks, I'd be glad to hear about it.

Anyway, I hope you enjoy finding your own – if 'enjoy' is always the right word, given that 'find your own' has more than one meaning. Here's one I found in an internet game played in 2019. I was playing the Black side and it's Black to play.

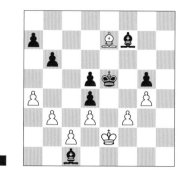

I found **36...♔f4!!**, the Worst Move On The Board. They're all there, waiting to be played.

Puzzle Selection

Find the Worst Move on the Board

position 1 – White to play

position 2 – Black to play

position 3 – White to play

position 4 – Black to play

position 5 – Black to play

position 6 – White to play

position 7 – Black to play

position 8 – Black to play

position 9 – Black to play

Solutions on page 104

DO YOU LIVE A BULLET LIFE, BLITZ LIFE, OR CLASSICAL LIFE?

Did I tell you I was running for President of the United States? No joke.

People would tell me (after hearing I did not vote), 'men died for your right to vote.' And this might be true. But they forget that the word 'right' means I have a choice to say 'no'.

I hope nobody died so I could be 'forced to vote'.

Or they would say, 'You shouldn't be allowed to have a voice if you didn't vote.' I don't know what authority they had to use the word 'should' but I figured I would one up them.

I did an experiment. I went to FEC.gov (the Federal Elections Commission in the US). I wanted to see how hard it was to officially run for President. The theory I was testing was that it was not very hard at all.

I filled out some online forms and now I am an official candidate for President of the United States in 2024. Now I guess I have 'a voice'.

I didn't have big fundraisers or go on talk shows or make speeches. That is the classical way to run for President.

I am 'bullet' running for President.

Vote for me.

■ ■ ■

I'm a big believer that the 10,000 hour rule (the idea that if you do something for 10,000 hours you will be the best in the world at it) is the road to misery.

Because if you do those 10,000 hours of deliberate practice (which means: doing something, having a coach look at it, repeat, for 10,000 hours) then afterwards you might say, 'Uh oh. That didn't work and I just wasted 20 years of my life!'

I believe in 10,000 experiments. Try things that you are curious about. Try them some more. Have a coach help you evaluate the results so you can tweak, and then experiment again.

You don't sit in a room for 10,000 hours practicing French. You go to France and try going to the bathroom. Try going to a restaurant. Try dating someone. Through experiment after experiment you learn French.

In 10,000 experiments you're either going to be great at a bunch of things, or at the very least you've had a very fun time and have many failures to laugh about.

I am experimenting with running for President of the United States.

By the way, I am also an honorary Colonel in the state of Kentucky (just like Muhammad Ali, Elvis Presley, and

> ## I'm a big believer that the 10,000 hour rule is the road to misery

Colonel Sanders, of Kentucky Fried Chicken fame). But that was another experiment.

However, if you see me in the street I wouldn't be so upset if you saluted.

■ ■ ■

My mission right now is to get back to my peak USCF rating of 2249 that I got in the 90s before quitting for 25 years.

I know that is not high to a lot of readers. But it's really important to me.

Everything turned upside down in the pandemic. People gave up jobs, careers, passions.

People felt lost and returned to old passions for some solace, for some sentiment, for some reclusive pleasure. For me, I want that great feeling of being able to consistently crush the souls of my opponents.

And it has been hard. Really, really difficult. I want to show I can get good again. What the brain has given with age can still be as good as what the brain has taken away.

And I want to improve quickly. Can I do it with 10,000 experiments (or preferably a 1000) instead of 10,000 hours?

So I ask a lot of grandmasters and coaches: is blitz chess good? Because I love blitz.

Many GMs say, 'Blitz will DO NOTHING to improve your play. You need to play classical games. That gives you the time to see the deeper ideas in a position. And then afterwards you can grow your chess by studying in depth.'

I remember reading that when Grischuk was younger he would do up to 20 pages of analysis or more for every classical game he played. I wanted to be like that.

But here is reality:

Magnus Carlsen has been a five-time world classical chess champion, a four-time world rapid chess champion, and a six-time world blitz chess champion.

And on chess.com his bullet rating is 3354. Out of 100,000,000+ players on chess.com he is number one with Hikaru number two.

What does this mean?

If you are good at one time control you are certainly good at the others.

It's not like Magnus is #1 in FIDE but rated 1900 in bullet on chess.com. You never heard Magnus Carlsen say, 'I'm the World Classical Chess Champion but I really wish I could play blitz chess as well as a 1700 player.'

They are all correlated.

If you are 2900 blitz on chess.com you are probably not a 1400 FIDE player. Improving at one, improves the other.

After talking to 100s of GMs/IMs/coaches/etc. here's what I have sort of concluded.

Classical

It's true that classical chess allows you to think more deeply into ideas. But what really happens is you have more time to calculate. I don't really think people come up with brand-new ideas while playing classical chess. They don't play g3 and then calculate that ♗g2 comes next. They already know this.

They get into the openings they have studied. Coming out of the opening they have already prepared the ideas and plans that they will focus on.

For instance, they get out of the opening in a Classical King's Indian as Black and know that they need to do ...f5, ...g5, ...f4, ...g4, ...♕h5, sac a bishop, checkmate.

The rest is calculation. Can they do ...g4 before the opponent does c5 and invades with ♖c7? At which exact point might they need to sacrifice a bishop? Unsure? Calculate.

When both sides have a lot of time, they get to the critical balancing edge of all of the ideas in the position and they start to calculate.

(Piket-Kasparov, Tilburg 1989, position after 20...g3, a perfect example of the Mar Del Plata Variation in the Classical King's Indian)

If you are 2900 blitz on chess. com you are probably not a 1400 FIDE player. Improving at one, improves the other

(If the above were a blitz game, I bet 95% of the moves would've been made in a second or less. This is the classic sort of position one might see in this variation.)

They already know the ideas and in classical chess they sit there and attempt to calculate one more further than the opponent to see if they can execute on those ideas.

Blitz chess

For someone like me: blitz chess is the laboratory of chess ideas. This is where I can experiment.

Sure, I can learn an opening by reading a book or looking at a few games. But the best way to learn is to DO something. I have to experiment to make sure I understand the ideas.

Every time you start calculating, you use valuable seconds. Calculation is the death of your blitz chess.

If one knows the ideas of a position, you can move without thinking (other than a blunder-check).

If I'm in a French, I might do ...c5 without thinking. And then maybe ...♛b6, ...♝d7, ...♝b5 if the opponent lets me and try to trade off that evil light-squared bishop.

If I'm in an isolated queen's pawn situation out of a Tarrasch maybe I try to trade off the minor pieces, double my rooks on the isolated queen's pawn and do c4 at the right moment when the d pawn is pinned, winning the pawn.

The only main tactic I hopefully will have to calculate is whether c3-c4 at the right moment wins that d-pawn.

All of this requires I know the ideas of the opening.

If my opponent knows the ideas better than me **then he will move faster,** playing the moves that execute on his ideas, and then at the right moment, spend a few extra seconds finding the two-three move tactic that crushes me.

I will have to calculate more to search for ideas. And then I will lose on time.

And, yes, he would probably beat me in classical as well.

Blitz is the training ground for the opening and the middle-games that result from those openings.

I try to keep disciplined. Playing six games a day at 5+3 (5 minutes + 3 second increment) I then analyze them myself, noting where I started to get confused as to what the right plan was, and then analyze them with a coach (GM Avetik Grigoryan).

In the space of a few hours, he quickly goes through the 40 or so games with me, tweaking each opening, showing me more ideas, fixing my thinking where I didn't execute on the ideas correctly, answering my questions, and so on.

I put everything into an increasingly big file and constantly review them.

'If we just went through the classical games you play, it would take years to go through the ideas in the openings', he told me.

The more plans you are familiar with in each opening, the faster you will move. French? Do ...c5! Mar Del Plata King's Indian? Organize ...f5! Ruy Lopez, depending on the variation, do ♞d2-f1-g3!

No thinking! No calculating.

If you lose, you figure out why ...c5 didn't work this time, make note of it, and move on.

It seems to be blitz is the best way to improve and then classical cements that improvement.

Bullet!

You know what the most winning move after 1.e4 g6 2.d4 ♝g7 is in bullet?

According to the Lichess database: 3. ♝h6 wins for White 67% of the time for players under 1500 even though it simply hangs a bishop. ♝h6 is a blunder but provokes a bigger blunder.

Because 70% of the time black does not take the bishop and blunders their own bishop. In other words, blunders decide the game almost instantly.

It has nothing to do with ideas or plans. Nothing to do with tactics. 'Aren't blunders, tactics?' No, because if you look at the

position and say 'Black to move and win', a 400 rated player can tell you ♝xh6 wins.

I said 1500 above. But when I tried to see at what level ♝h6 is not the most successful move I tried 1600... 1800.. 2000... 2200...... It's only when I look at players 2500 and above that the win rate for ♝h6 goes below 50%!

In other words, 2500s blunder less. Bullet is the laboratory of blunders. Experiment with ways to avoid blunders and your bullet will improve.

As you weed blunders out of your bullet play, your blitz play will get better.

And if you know more ideas in your opening and middle games and know the ideas behind all the basic technical endgames, your blitz will greatly improve. Which means your classical will improve.

And if you are great at calculating and have knowledge of many plans (as studied in blitz), your classical will improve even more.

It seems to be blitz is the best way to improve and then classical cements that improvement

But can't you improve all of this with just classical?

Sure, play two to five classical games a week and study them. Or play 50 blitz games a week and study them. Which approach will teach you more plans that come out of your openings?

Quantity of plans is key.

■ ■ ■

In summary, vote James Altucher for President in 2024.

I promise I will eliminate all of your taxes and will mandate peace and happiness throughout the world. Or, at least, I will experiment with ways of doing that. ■

MAXIMize your Tactics

with Maxim Notkin

Find the best move in the positions below

Solutions on page 93

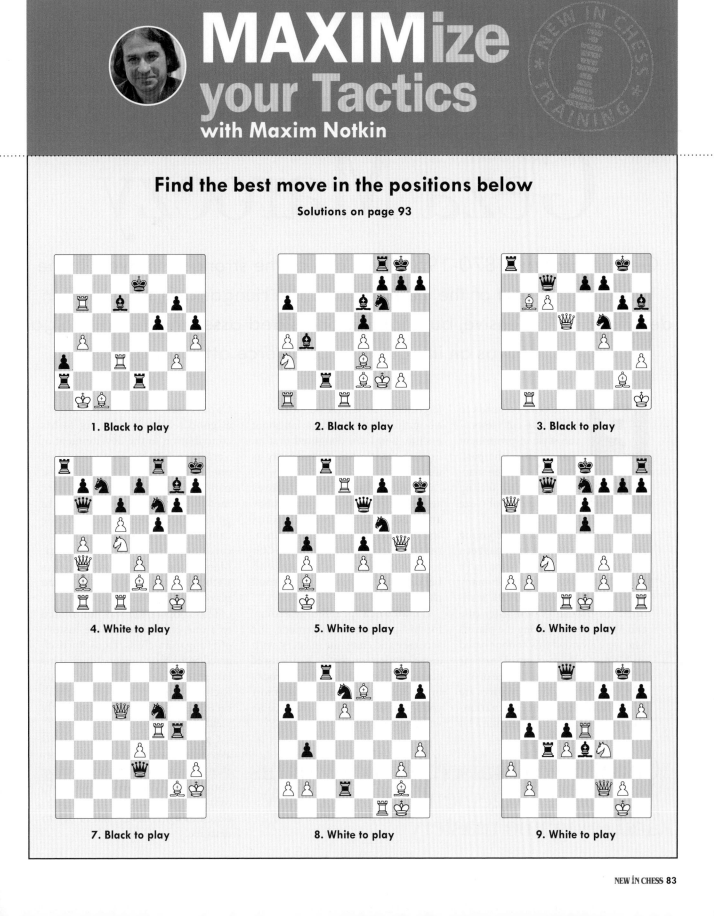

1. Black to play

2. Black to play

3. Black to play

4. White to play

5. White to play

6. White to play

7. Black to play

8. White to play

9. White to play

Judit Polgar

In defence of Geza Maroczy

Geza Maroczy (1870-1951) was one of the strongest players in the world at the start of the 20th century. The Hungarian's style is often described as defensive, but that is a one-sided assessment, Judit Polgar argues. He was an imaginative and fierce attacker as well.

Public opinion tends to hold clear-cut views of the style of prominent players from the past, but these judgements are often inaccurate. I clearly have this feeling about the 'official portrait' of Geza Maroczy.

For many generations of young Hungarian players, Maroczy has been a role model. Born in 1870, he had a prodigious career filled with many great victories. In 1950, FIDE instituted the official grandmaster title and Maroczy was among the players who were awarded this honour based on his past achievements. One year later, he passed away at the age of 81.

In Hungary, various initiatives are named after him, but internationally, Maroczy may have become a bit forgotten. 2021 saw the publication of a beautiful book in Hungarian about his life, and I am delighted that an English translation is on its way as well.

Maroczy had positive scores against players like Euwe, Bogoljubov and Réti, but had modest results against Alekhine and Capablanca. In 1906, he agreed on the terms for a world championship match with Lasker, but the match never took place.

Capablanca praised Maroczy for his positional judgement, his accuracy and endgame mastery, with a special mention for his handling of queen endings, adding that Maroczy in his prime was stronger than most young players around at the time he wrote his comments.

Capablanca also called Maroczy a 'good teacher', referring to his contribution to the development of Vera Menchik, but there is at least one more example. Before his first match with Alekhine, Max Euwe met with Maroczy in Vienna, to go through Professor Becker's file cabinet, which contained 15,000 cards with games. Prior to that, Maroczy had already prepared files with all the games Alekhine had played over the past 10 years.

This cooperation was not limited to a one-off episode in the history of Hungarian chess. Lajos Portisch acted as Karpov's second during his last match against Kasparov, while Richard Rapport was Ding Liren's second in the match that recently yielded him the world title.

Capablanca rightly felt that his assessment was still missing something, but came up with the wrong conclusion. According to him, Maroczy 'was lacking in imagination and aggressive spirit'. I beg to disagree.

Capablanca praised Maroczy for his positional judgement, his accuracy and endgame mastery

Geza Maroczy had close ties with Max Euwe and often visited the Netherlands.
Here 'veteran' Maroczy (66) faces young star Reuben Fine (21) at the tournament in Zandvoort in 1936.

Trademark 1 – imagination

The truth is that Maroczy's play frequently featured daring sacrifices and attacks. To give an example of his rich imagination, I have selected a game that he played at the age of 60.

Geza Maroczy
Massimiliano Romi
San Remo 1930

position after 38...♖h8

Earlier in the game, White had had a crushing attack, but he lost the thread and spoiled everything. In the current position, he does not have

any compensation for the bishop and should lose.

Maroczy decided to sell his skin dearly. His next two moves require accurate answers from Black if he wants to win, but as we will see, the play goes on for three results!

39.e7+!
This pawn is more dangerous than it may look.

39...♔e8!
39...♔xe7? loses quickly to 40.♖g7+. The king is also misplaced after 39...♔d7? 40.♖e1, threatening 41. e8♕+ ♖xe8 42.♕h7+ and mating soon. 40...♖e8 (40...♔e8 loses a tempo with respect to the game variation; one of the winning moves is 41.♖g7!, cutting off the communication between the black queen and the h8-rook: 41...♖xh6 42.♖g8+ ♔d7 43.e8♕+ ♔c7 44.♕xc8+ ♔b6 45.♖e7 winning) 41.♖g8! ♖xg8 42.♕e6+ ♔c7 43.♕xg8, and Black cannot prevent the pawn from queening, for instance 43...♗d7 44.♕d8+ ♔d6 45.e8♕, and the bishop is pinned.
39...♔c7? is safer than the contin-

uations above, but does not offer winning chances.

40.♖e1!
Maroczy calmly tightens the net around the enemy king. We had this position in the second variation above, but with White to move. Black now has a tempo for parrying the threats of ♖g7 and ♖f6.

40...♖d2? Played with the intention of freeing himself with ...♖xg2!+, which also parries the initial threats. However, it offers White a new possibility.
40...♗xh3!? would have been only enough for equality: 41.♖e2! ♕c3

42.gxh3 ♖d3 43.♖g8+ ♖xg8 44.♕h5+ ♔d7 45.e8♕+ ♖xe8 46.♕xe8+ ♔c7 47.♕e5+, with a probable draw.

The only winning move was 40...♖d3! 41.♖g8+!? (both 41.♖g7 and 41.♖f6 run into 41...♖xh3+!) 41...♖xg8 42.♕h5+ ♔d7 43.e8♕+ ♖xe8 44.♕h7+ ♔d8 45.♕xd3+ ♗d7. After giving up the advanced pawn, White does not have any compensation for the bishop.

41.♕h5!! What a shock! The queen remains under the rook's attack and creates a lethal battery along the h5-e8 diagonal. The threat of a discovered check is devastating. As shown by the game continuation, the last move also takes measures against the capture on g2.

Such a move is easy to miss. We cannot know when exactly Maroczy foresaw this fantastic move, but we can say that he displayed quite a bit of imagination when playing it, thus contradicting Capablanca.

41...♖xg2+ In the event of 41...♔d7, the shortest win is 42.e8♕+! ♖xe8 43.♕h7+ ♔d8 44.♖xe8+ ♔xe8 45.♖g8 mate.

42.♖xg2+ With check! **42...♖xh5 43.♖xb2**

The rest is simple. **43...♖xh3+ 44.♔g1** Keeping the second rank clear for the rook. **44...♖h7 45.♖h2 ♖g7+** 45...♖xe7 46.♖h8+ wins the bishop. **46.♔f2 ♖g8 47.♖h6 ♔f7 48.e8♕+ ♖xe8 49.♖h7+** 1-0.

Capablanca was not the only expert to ignore the creative side of Maroczy's style. Most sources describe him as a defensive player. In their book series *The Middlegame*, Euwe and Kramer used several games played by Maroczy, as examples of accurate defending. While all this may be true, the following game offers a strong contrast.

Trademark 2 – Relentless attacker
In the next example, Maroczy defeated his mighty opponent, a former world title challenger and renowned romantic player, with his own weapons.

As a child, I was delighted to see games like this, in which one player would sacrifice one or two pieces for the attack. I played the King's Gambit myself, but mainly with 3.♗c4.

Geza Maroczy
Mikhail Chigorin
Vienna 1903
King's Gambit, McDonnell Gambit

1.e4 e5 2.f4
Quite a brave move for a 'defensive player'. True, this game was played in a King's Gambit Accepted theme tournament, where this opening was prescribed, but Maroczy used the King's Gambit more than 15 times in regular competitions, too.
2...exf4 3.♘f3 g5 4.♗c4 g4

This move had been known since Greco played this line with both colours in the first part of the 17th century.

5.♘c3 This was the favourite continuation of Alexander McDonnell, who used it regularly, also in several games of his matches against Labourdonnais. Known since the 18th century, 5.0-0 is a by far more popular way of sacrificing the knight. It occasionally still pops up in top-level blitz games. For instance, 5...gxf3 6.♕xf3 ♗h6?! 7.d4, with huge compensation for the piece, was seen in Nakamura-Andreikin, Moscow World Blitz Championship 2010.
5...gxf3 6.♕xf3 d6 7.d4 ♗e6 8.♘d5 c6 9.0-0 cxd5 10.exd5

As a kid, I learned about the incredible power of the initiative. The main idea of the King's Gambit is to sacrifice material for the sake of speeding up development.
10...♗f5 11.♗xf4 ♗g6?!
The bishop was exposed on f5, but White could have exploited it only by attacking it. He preferred a developing move instead.

12.♗b5+
White has entirely adequate compen-

sation for the sacrificed knights now.

12...♘d7 13.♖ae1+ ♗e7

Black had a difficult choice.

13...♘e7 was a viable alternative, with the possible continuation 14.♗xd6 ♕b6 15.♗xd7+ ♔xd7 16.♗c5 ♕a6 17.d6, with unclear play. Black has to return some material, since 17...♘c6? would allow White to win with 18.♕h3+ f5 19.♖xf5!,

14.♗xd6

14...♔f8

The king will not find absolute safety on the kingside, but the only other possible move, 14...♕b6, also yields White a strong initiative: 15.c4!! (sacrificing the third piece, at least temporarily) 15...♕xd6 (the king is not entirely safe on the queenside, either: 15...0-0-0 16.♗xd7+ ♖xd7 17.♗e5, followed by c4-c5-c6, with a dangerous initiative) 16.c5 ♕f6 17.♕c3, followed by d5-d6, maintaining the attack.

15.♖xe7! Retrieving part of the material. **15...♘xe7 16.♖e1 ♔g7 17.♗xe7**

17...♕a5! An important move, gaining a tempo by attacking the rook and the bishop.

17...♕c7 18.♗xd7 ♕xd7 19.♗f6+ paralyses Black.

18.♕e2

18...♘f8? This passive move leads to a quick defeat.

Black should have completed the regrouping initiated by ...♔f8 with 18...♖hd8! 19.c4 (the most consistent move, defending d5) 19...h6! (clearing the h7-square for the king, in anticipation of ♗xd7, followed by ♗f6+; 19...h5 is also good) 20.b4 ♕a3!

(all moves followed by an exclamation mark are forced. After 20...♕c7?, 21.d6 ♕c8 22.c5 is crushing, despite Black's extra rook) 21.♗xd8 ♖xd8 22.♕e7 (Black's pieces are hanging, but he can develop enough counterplay) 22...♕c3! 23.♖f1 ♕xd4+! 24.♔h1 ♗d3! (forcing the rook to leave either the f2-square or the first rank undefended; it is essential to keep the queen on d4: after 24...♕d3?, 25.♖g1 ♘f6 26.♕xd8 ♘g4 27.♕h4 parries the threats, maintaining a

decisive material advantage) 25.♖xf7+! ♔g6 26.h3 ♕a1+ 27.♔h2 ♕e5+ 28.♕xe5 ♘xe5 29.♖xb7 ♗c4 30.♗xc4 ♘xc4 31.♖xa7, with a probable draw.

This long piece of analysis illustrates the number of practical problems lying ahead for Black, even if he had spotted the correct 18th move.

19.♗f6+ Even if Chigorin had overlooked this move, his oversight remains curious, since 19.♕e5+ ♔g8 20.♗f6 would have transposed to the game.

19...♔g8 19...♔xf6 would run into 20.♕e5, mate. **20.♕e5 h6 21.♗xh8 f6 22.♕e7 ♔xh8 23.♕xf6+**

Seeing 23...♔g8 24.♖e7, Black resigned.

Conclusions:

■ A rich imagination can be a determining quality in positions with hidden resources that only need to be uncovered.

■ One should trust the power of the initiative and not shy away from sacrificing material in order to grab it. ■

Trust the power of the initiative and do not shy away from sacrificing material in order to grab it

NEW IN CHESS
B O O K S

Practical and Creative Lessons for Amateurs
Boris Zlotnik

Boris Zlotnik, the former coach of U.S. Champion Fabiano Caruana, offers practical chess lessons for amateurs about highly original subjects like creativity or 'putting up resistance' – topics seldom touched on in other chess manuals. Zlotnik covers a wide variety of topics and uses a wealth of material in an extraordinarily instructive chess manual.

The unbeaten grandmaster
Sergei Tiviakov

Sergei Tiviakov was unbeaten for a consecutive 110 professional chess games as a grandmaster. Who better to teach you rock-solid chess strategy than Tiviakov? In his first book, he explains everything he knows about the fundamentals of chess strategy: pawn structures.

The Rivalry between Steinitz and Zukertort
Willy Hendriks

The rivalry between William Steinitz and Johannes Zukertort, the world's strongest chess players in the late nineteenth century, became so fierce that it was named 'The Ink War'. Who was the strongest player? And who had the best ideas? In *The Ink War*, IM Willy Hendriks once again offers his unique perspective on the birth of modern chess.

Another Hit Repertoire by Sielecki
Christof Sielecki

Christof Sielecki presents a complete solution to chess players of all levels for their opening choices with the black pieces. With this repertoire, you will safely navigate the opening phase and understand what is happening and how you can play for a win. Yes, it is simple but not boring!

Training for Club Players (1800-2100)
Davorin Kuljasevic

The success of the book *How To Study Chess on Your Own* made clear that thousands of chess players want to improve their game. This Workbook gets you started immediately. Kuljasevic has used his coaching experience to create a broad and exciting training schedule.

Sharpen your endgame tactics
Thomas Willemze

In *1001 Chess Endgame Exercises for Beginners*, IM Thomas Willemze does two things simultaneously. He explains all the basic concepts and provides many exercises for each theme and each chess piece in a highly instructive puzzle rush.

The fourth volume of the *1001 Exercises* series.

Chess.com 2022 Book of the Year
Ramesh RB

Coach Ramesh has won the *2022 Chess.com Book of the Year Award*, in a vote with thousands of chess players. It is well deserved. But beware! It is a tough book that will require some real effort. Are you up for the challenge?

"An absolute divine masterpiece" – *Andras Toth*.

Kavalek's long-awaited memoir
Lubomir Kavalek

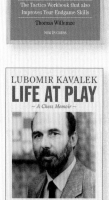

American-Czech Grandmaster Lubomir Kavalek (1943-2021) was a three-time US Chess Champion and one of the best chess writers of the last decades. Kavalek could speak from experience as he worked with or met all the chess greats of the last century, from Bobby Fischer to Nigel Short. Including many of his best games with Kavalek's entertaining comments.

The oldest chess tournament in the world
Jürgen Brustkern & Norbert Wallet

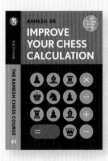

No other chess tournament has such a long and rich history as Hastings. Countless chess players, professionals and amateurs alike, have celebrated Christmas and welcomed the New Year in Hastings while battling it out on the chessboard. The book covers the tournament's fascinating history and portrays forty of the most colourful participants. The stories begin in 1895 and span 125 years.

A brilliant new endgame manual
Herman Grooten

The author of the bestsellers *Chess Strategy for Club Players* and *Attacking Chess for Club Players* finally explains how to play the endgame. He shows how to understand themes or patterns and for example tells you how to cut off the enemy king or create a passed pawn – and win many more endgames.

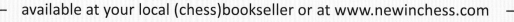

Thomas Willemze

Club players, test your decision-making skills!

What would you play?

Streamers mostly work from home, but at times they also play in tournaments. To feel the excitement of in-person chess, meet fans and, of course, to keep streaming!

L ast April, I participated in the 2023 Reykjavik Open – a popular tournament that reserved a separate corner for a group of well-known streamers to share their live-games with their fans. I was impressed to see how these professionals could focus on their games while staying in tune with the many chess enthusiasts in between the rounds.

I have selected one of the games of **Alexandra Botez**, the popular American-Canadian streamer with more than a million followers, and created four exercises in which you can think along with her. It was a complex game, in which her opponent, **Steven Wollkind**, had to show active piece play to compensate for his damaged pawn structure.

I hope you will enjoy these exercises and will be able to uncover the tactical opportunities for both players. You can find the full analysis of this game on the pages below.

Exercise 1

position after 15...♗h3

Black's last move was aimed at preventing his opponent from castling. **What would you play?** Create a safe spot for your king with **16.f3**, or trade the annoying dark-squared bishop with **16.♘a2** ?

Exercise 2

position after 20...axb4

The game has just entered a new phase after the queen swap. How would you deal with the attack on the a4-pawn? Protect it with **21.b3** or push it with **21.a5** ?

Exercise 3

position after 31...♖a8

White has a large advantage in this ending, but the game is not over yet. What would be the most precise move for her to play?

Exercise 4

position after 39...♖b7

White found a pretty way to decide the game at once. Can you spot it?

Alexandra Botez (1988)
Steven Wollkind (1345)
Reykjavik Open 2023
Queen's Gambit Declined

**1.d4 d5 2.♘f3 ♘f6 3.c4 e6 4.♘c3
a6**

This quiet move has become very popular over the last couple of years. The 'threat' of 5...dxc4, followed by 6...b5, should convince White of the wisdom to release the tension in the centre.

5.cxd5 exd5 6.♗g5 ♗e6

7.♗xf6 gxf6

It was unnecessary to weaken the pawn structure voluntarily. Black probably feared 7...♕xf6 8.♕b3, with a double attack on b7 and d5. However, the theory shows that Black is fine after 8...♖a7!, since 9.♘xd5 will be met by the powerful exchange sacrifice 9...♕d8! 10.e4 c6!.

ANALYSIS DIAGRAM

Black is in good shape after 11.♕b6 cxd5! 12.♕xa7 dxe4.

8.♕b3 ♘d7 9.e3

9.♕xb7 ♘b6! favours Black, because the white queen will be stuck on b7 for the time being.

9...♗d6 10.g3!

Good endgame technique brought
Alexandra Botez the win.

White shows excellent technique by **placing her pawns on the dark squares** to complement the remaining light-squared bishop. The e3/g3-setup also prevents Black from resolving the ugly doubled f-pawn with ...f6-f5-f4.

10...♘b6 11.a4 a5 12.♖d1

It will soon become clear that the rook was already useful on a1, protecting the a4-pawn. **Improving the worst placed piece** with 12.♗d3! was the way to go. The annoying 12...♗h3 can be met by 13.♘h4! ♗b4 14.♗f5.

12...♗b4 13.♘d2

Developing the bishop was still White's main priority, even though Black gets enough activity to com-

pensate for his poor pawn structure after 13.♗g2 ♕d7 14.♖a1 h5.

13...♕d7

14.♗b5

This is where White could use the rook on a1, as the bishop has to spend an extra tempo to keep the a4-pawn alive now.

14...c6 15.♗e2 ♗h3

This annoying move prevents White from castling kingside and leads to **Exercise 1**.

16.f3

This was a tough decision! We were taught to **complete our development** before taking any action, and connecting the rooks with ♔f2 feels like a very natural plan. We should remember, however, that White was using her pawns to replace the dark-squared bishop, with the **f2-pawn as a rock-solid base**. Pushing this pawn jeopardizes both e3 and g3, and ultimately the king. It would therefore have been wiser to leave the king on e1 for the moment and focus on the queenside instead.

The right answer was 16.♘a2! ♗xd2+ 17.♖xd2, after which White should improve the knight with ♘c1-d3 and get a level game.

16...h5 This logical move is too hasty. It was important to protect the knight first with 16...♕c7! and prepare ...♗d6 to attack the g3-pawn once more. Black is clearly better after 17.♘a2 ♗d6 18.♔f2 0-0-0.

ANALYSIS DIAGRAM

Note how Black has a clear plan with ...h7-h5-h4, whereas White will find it difficult to create something similar on the queenside.
17.♔f2 17.♘a2! would still be the best option for White.
17...0-0-0
And this was the last opportunity to get a large advantage with 17...♕c7. It is now White's turn to take action.

18.♘a2!
This move has become even stronger with the black king castled queenside.
18...♕d6
18...♗xd2 19.♕xb6 is terrible for Black.
19.♘xb4 ♕xb4 20.♕xb4 axb4

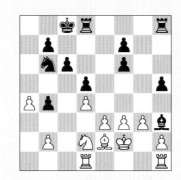

21.b3
This move protects the vulnerable c4-square, but is a bit slow and, more importantly, blocks the white knight. The aggressive 21.a5! was the solution to **Exercise 2**. White gets a large advantage after 21...♘d7 22.♘b3 ♔c7 23.♖a1, followed by ♖a4 and/or ♘c1-d3.
21...♗f5

Black gives his opponent a second chance to develop a powerful initiative on the queenside. Improving the knight with 21...♔b8! 22.a5 ♘c8 and ...♘d6 would have kept the game level.
22.a5! ♘d7 23.♖a1 ♔c7

24.♖a4!
This is what White was aiming for. The b4-pawn is about to drop.
24...♖a8 25.♖ha1 b5 26.axb6+ ♘xb6

27.♖a7+
Very thematic. Rooks belong on the 7th rank!
27...♔d6 28.♖1a6 ♖xa7 29.♖xa7

29...♗g6

Sacrificing the f7-pawn with 29...♖a8 looks tempting, but a closer look reveals that the minor piece ending that arises after 30.♖xa8! ♘xa8 puts White in total control. She can easily improve her position with 31.e4! ♗g6 32.♔e3!, followed by f4-f5, while Black is stuck with uncoordinated pieces.

30.♖b7 ♘d7 31.♖xb4 ♖a8

32.♖a4!

Well played! This was the right answer to **Exercise 3**. White does not fear the minor piece ending and blocks the a-file to keep the enemy rook passive.

32...♖b8 33.h4

Botez steered the game into a favourable ending where she displayed an impeccable technique

Fixing the enemy pawns on their bishop's colour might always prove useful later.

33...♗c2 34.♖a3 f5 35.♖a7!

The rook returns to its beloved 7th rank. White has already seen that the pawn sacrifice is only temporary.

35...♗xb3

36.♗d3!

White is, of course, not interested in trading her beautiful knight for the dark-squared bishop.

36...♔e6 37.♖a6

This is what White was aiming at. The black rook is still occupied defending the bishop, and either the f5- or the c6-pawn is about to drop.

37...♔d6 38.♗xf5 ♗c2

Black shows the right fighting spirit and tries to complicate the game with this temporary piece sacrifice.

39.e4!

Simple and strong. 39.♗xc2 ♖b2 was Black's idea.

39...♖b7

The key to **Exercise 4** was to recognize that White's 39.e4 has created a **battery**, consisting of a **rear piece** (the bishop) and a **front piece** (the

e4-pawn). This tactical devise enables White to execute a **discovered attack** in which the front piece attacks the first target and opens the diagonal for the rear piece to attack a second piece.

40.e5+!

White found this decisive combination on the last move before the time-control. The e-pawn gives a check and simultaneously opens up the b1-h7 diagonal for the bishop. The result is a **double attack** on both the king and the bishop. Black cannot parry both threats at once and loses a piece.

Note that discovered attacks in which the rear piece attacks its target in a **backwards direction** are quite rare, which may have been the reason why Black missed it under time-pressure.

40...♔e7

40...♔c7 wouldn't have saved Black either in view of 41.♗xc2 ♖b2

ANALYSIS DIAGRAM

42.♖a7+! ♔d8 43.♗f5! ♘b8 44.♔e1.

41.♗xc2 ♘b8 41...♖b2 is now refuted by the simple 42.♖xc6.

42.♖a2 Black resigned.

Conclusion

Kudos to Black for fighting himself back into the game with a severely wounded pawn structure. The game could have ended differently if he had prepared the march of his h-pawn with the precise 16...♕c7! and ...♗d6. White did not allow her opponent a second chance, as she immediately steered the game into a favourable endgame, in which she displayed impeccable technique and decided the game with a pretty discovered attack. ∎

MAXIMize your Tactics Solutions

1. Pijpers-Garrido
Alicante 2023

43...♖a1+! 44.♔xa1 ♗e5+ 45.♔b2 If 45.♔b1, 45...a2 mate. **45...axb2+ 46.♔a2 ♖e1 47.♖b3** Hastening the end. After 47.♖b7+ ♔f6 the king escapes to h6. **47...♖a1** Mate.

2. Druska-Macieja
Ledyard 2023

23...♘xg4+! 23...♘xe4+ just transposes. **24.fxg4 ♖xe2+! 25.♔xe2 ♗xg4+ 26.♔f2 ♗xd1 27.♖xd1 ♗xa3** and with two extra pawns Black went on to win.

3. Sanket-Johansson
Fagernes 2023

35...♕xb6! 35...♖xf4 36.c7 is less vigorous. White resigned in view of 36.♖xb6 ♖a1+ 37.♗f1 (37.♔h2 ♗xf4 mate) 37...♖xf1+ 38.♔g2 ♘e3+.

4. Kazhgaleyev-Gareev
Tashkent 2022

21.♘xf5! White wins a pawn as in case of 21...gxf5 22.♗d4 the queen is trapped. Black tried **21...e5 22.dxe6 gxf5** but after **23.♗d4 ♕c6 24.♖dc1** he resigned anyway.

5. Jumabayev-Grover
Dubai 2022

42.♖d6! As 42...♖xd6 43.♕g7 is mate. And 42...♖g8 43.♖xe6 ♖xg4 44.hxg4 fxe6 45.gxf5 costs a piece. **42...♕xd6 43.♕xf5+ ♕g6 44.♕xc8** and White soon won.

6. Lenderman-Jia Haoxiang
Titled Tuesday 2022

17.♘b5 ♕c6 The only way to try and save the exchange. **18.♘d6+ ♔f8 19.♘xc8!** Black resigned as 19...♖xa6 20.♖d8 is checkmate.

7. Gullaksen-Alsina
Barcelona 2022

35...♖xg2+! 36.♔xg2 ♕xe4+ 37.♔f3 It may seem that White got off lightly but **37...♕e2+** forced him to resign as after 38.♖f2 ♕xf2+! 39.♔xf2 ♘e4+ Black would be a piece up.

8. Poliannikov-S.Sethuraman
New York 2022

31.♗h3 ♖cc2 32.♗e6+ ♔h8 If 32...♔g7 33.♖f7+ ♔h6 34.♗g5+ ♔h5 35.♖xh7 mate. **33.♖f8+!** Now 33...♔g7 34.♖g8+ ♔h6 35.♗g5+ ♔h5 36.g4 is mate. Black preferred to go down in style. **33...♘xf8 34.♗f6** Mate.

9. Le Tuan Minh-C. Cruz
Titled Tuesday 2022

35.♘xd5! ♖c1+ 35...f5 36.♖e8+! ♕xe8 37.♘f6+ loses the queen. Both 35...♔f8 and 35...♖c2 run into 36.♕f6! **36.♔h2 ♗xd5 37.♕f6! ♕b8** Avoiding 37...♕xf6 38.♖e8 mate or 37...♕f8 38.♖e8 and forgetting about... **38.♕g7** Mate.

Rational and irrational chess

Beauty can have many faces. Matthew Sadler shares his enthusiasm about books dedicated to solid iron logic, breath-taking mayhem and the serene heights of problem-solving.

I was chatting with Michael Adams recently during a dinner and we started to discuss the process of analysing positions with engines and annotating games. He made the funny but very astute observation that what engines say is often not very useful but unfortunately you can't ignore what they say either, so you end up not really knowing what to do! For example, you ideally want to generalise key moments in game annotations to provide the reader with knowledge that can be reused in subsequent games. Engines have a way of crossing this goal, most often by highlighting a series of specific exceptions to the narrative you are trying to build. It can cost a substantial amount of effort to discover the reason a specific exception works...

and then you still need to figure out how to explain this succinctly to your readers, or whether it's even possible without confusing them! Ideally, tools should simplify your work, but engines – even for the highest-level players – can complicate as much as they help!

For all that, I remain very positive about the value of chess engines in chess improvement, but I think it's clear that working optimally with engines requires more subtlety and thought than you might expect.

From that point of view, I would recommend the introductory chapter of Sergei Tiviakov's & Yulia Gökbulut's *Rock Solid Chess* (New In Chess) to everyone to read. The chapter is entitled 'Human chess versus computer chess' and was apparently added to the book after some feedback on the original manuscript. I'm somewhat intrigued as to the nature of this feedback as the rest seemed excellent to me anyway, but the chapter definitely adds an extra dimension to the book. Sergei runs through a series of positions in which an engine discovers hidden possibilities or improves on human play, and gives his opinion on which are valuable for human learning – and how to make use of them – and which should be put aside.

Interestingly, this last category includes a typical Italian game position from one of Sergei's games:

Sergei Tiviakov
Gilberto Milos
Tromsø Olympiad 2014
1.e4 e5 2.♘f3 ♘c6 3.♗c4 ♗c5 4.c3 ♘f6 5.d3 a6 6.♗b3 ♗a7 7.h3 0-0 8.♗g5 d6 9.♘h2 h6 10.♗h4 g5 11.♗g3 ♘e7 12.h4 ♘g6 13.hxg5 hxg5 14.♘d2 ♔g7 15.♕e2

Sergei's comments are worth quoting in full: 'Question: What are the human and computer assessments of the position? As far as I'm concerned, White has

Ideally, tools should simplify your work, but engines – even for the highest-level players – can complicate as much as they help!

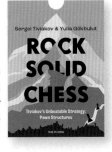

Rock Solid Chess
Sergei Tiviakov &
Yulia Gökbulut
New In Chess, 2023
★★★★★

the advantage: it's easier for him to play. But the computer, you will be surprised, goes for Black. It is not embarrassed by serious pawn defects in the position, weakened squares, as well as pawn thrusts which have exposed its own king, like 10... g5. For it, this is absolutely normal play. The engine's defence is based on dynamics, on specific move-by-move play. It is extremely difficult for a human to play such positions. You should consider this when preparing for an opponent.'

And indeed, Sergei won a game in which an engine-free glance would not detect anything else than a slight Black disadvantage from this position on!

I loved this chapter as an exposition of how an understanding of engines' play can broaden your game – either by opening your mind to generalisable possibilities of which you had not dreamt, or by allowing you to ignore engine evaluations which would require an elevated level of accuracy from your opponents which they could never sustain!

It's obviously natural for me to focus on the chapter that intersects with my chess passion at the moment, but that wouldn't do justice to the rest of the book, which is excellent too. Anyone who has prepared for Sergei can't help but be struck at the number of systems he played that scorned conventional evaluation. Many of his White systems – for example against the French, Sicilian and Caro-Kann – aimed for a simple structure (such as 3 vs 2 on the queenside), which he then exploited to perfection through superior understanding. He was the

type of player – Michael Adams is another – who made you nervous about heading for supposedly 'equal' positions out of the opening against them!

Quite appropriately, the book's seven chapters are organised around typical structures that Sergei reached in his games. Of these, the very first – 'Pawn majority on one flank' – is my favourite, containing opening, middlegame and endgame insights on the pawn structures that have been Sergei's bread and butter throughout his whole career.

It's a really excellent book, not heavy in variations, easy to read and full of advanced but well-formulated advice. I'd recommend it unreservedly to any (young) player who wishes to enrich their understanding of the game. Five well-deserved stars!

■ ■ ■

Cyrus Lakdawala's *Irrational Chess* (Everyman) is the type of book that you close with a thump at the end and exclaim 'I'm not sure what I learnt from that, but it was a fun ride!' In eight chapters (with titles such as 'Attack', 'Irrational Endings', 'Opening Shockers' and 'Promotion

Lakdawala takes us on a helter-skelter journey through the craziest games and positions ever seen!

Races') and 400 pages, Lakdawala takes us on a helter-skelter journey through the craziest games and positions ever seen! The first chapter gathers together a lot of familiar (though always welcome) classics such as Polugaevsky-Nezhmetdinov, Sochi 1958, and Tal-Keller, Zurich 1959, but events take a turn on the wild side as we head into the following chapters. There was a series of games in the 'The Dynamic

Irrational Chess
Cyrus Lakdawala
Everyman, 2023
★★★★☆

Element' chapter that I particularly enjoyed, both for the spectacle and for the fact that they were unknown to me! Take this astonishing brawl between Bent Larsen and David Bronstein at Moscow 1962.

Bent Larsen
David Bronstein
Moscow 1962

position after 27.♕h4

Bronstein had sacrificed a pawn nine moves earlier, to slow down White's attack through the exchange of White's light-squared bishop and – still faced with kingside pressure – he had no hesitation in offering another pawn to make his kingside light squares still safer!

27...g5!! 28.♘xg5 ♗xg5
Lakdawala's comment here is typical of his style: 'Now Larsen is saddled with a terrible, rotten, no-good bishop, versus Bronstein's killer knight'!

**29.♕xg5+ ♔f7 30.♕h4 ♖g8
31.♖f3 ♖g4 32.♕f2 ♘g8**
Lakdawala describes here Black's full compensation for the two sacrificed pawns. This would be nice enough on its own, but the efforts that Larsen now makes to shake the foundations

of Black's position are pretty impressive, as is Bronstein's reaction!

33.♖xe4 dxe4 34.♖h3 ♘h6 35.♕e2 ♖g8 36.b3 As Lakdawala points out, 'Larsen plays for the full point. In doing so, he also risks a loss'.

36...cxb3 37.axb3 ♕d5 38.b4 ♕a2 39.♔f1 ♔e6 40.g3

40...♔d5 A scenario reminiscent of shogi, where penetrating to the opponent's side of the board with the king is normally a harbinger of victory! Bronstein seems to have the game sealed, but Larsen has other ideas!

41.♗e1 ♕b1 42.g4 ♖xg4 43.c4+

43...bxc4 44.♖a3 This was Larsen's idea: the sacrifice of the g- and c-pawns – at no small risk to his own position – has opened a path for his rook to give checks to the black king via the opposite flank! Great vision and even greater courage!

44...♖xf4+ 45.♔g2 ♖g4+ 46.♔h3 ♖f4 47.♖a5+ ♔xd4 The reality-defying best move! **48.♗f2+ ♖xf2 49.♕xf2+ e3 50.♕f4+ ♕e4 51.♕xe4+**

Lakdawala's comment is again very apt: 'You have to be kidding me. This is pure faith, rather than scientific

reason. There is no way Larsen could have calculated the consequence of the coming promotion race. The engine still says it's even. Every other player in the universe would have taken a draw: 51.♕xh6 ♕h1+ 52.♔g3 ♕g1+ 53.♔h3 ♕h1+, with perpetual check.'

51...♔xe4 52.♖xa6

52...e2? 'After playing such a brilliant game, Bronstein gets Charlie-Browned, where the position's Lucy pulls the football away at the last second. This is the wrong pawn push.'

53.♔g2 ♔d3 54.♔f2 ♘g4+ 55.♔e1 ♘e5 56.♖d6+ ♔e3 57.♖e6 ♔d4 58.h6 ♘d3+ 59.♔xe2 ♘f4+ 60.♔d1 ♘xe6 61.h7 1-0.

It's a fun read packed with games you won't feel sorry to have seen once in your life! It seemed somewhere between 3 and 4 stars to me but since the sun is out, we'll give it a sunny 4!

■ ■ ■

Pressure Play by English grandmaster Neil McDonald (Everyman) is perhaps the complete opposite, extolling the virtues of tight positional play to squeeze errors from the opponent and grind him into submission! Chapters such as 'Paralysing the Enemy Pieces', 'Targeting the Weakest Squares on the Board' and 'Increasing and Exploiting a Space Advantage' give a flavour of the seriousness of the content! One nice element is the mixture of games that McDonald finds to illustrate his themes: old and modern, amateur and elite. For example, this example early in the book by the English amateur Cliff Chandler is quite something!

McDonald suggests that one of the differences between players of the 1980s and 2020s is that 'nowadays players are more willing to take liberties with the safety of their king to achieve positional aims'

Clifford Chandler (2246)
Kevin Bowmer (2100)
Kenilworth Chessable Seniors
65+ 2022
Sicilian Defence

1.e4 c5 2.a3 e6 3.b4 cxb4 4.axb4 ♗xb4 5.♗b2 ♗f8

6.♖a3 The first exchange offer cannot be accepted, as 6...♗xa3 7.♗xg7 is strong for White.

6...♘c6 7.♖g3 ♘f6 8.e5 ♘e4 9.♖e3 ♘c5 10.♘f3 ♘a4 11.♗a1 ♘b6 12.♘c3 ♗c5

13.♘e4 This second offer is just as

powerful! **13...♗xe3 14.♘d6+ ♔f8 15.fxe3 f5 16.♗d3 g6 17.0-0 ♔g7 18.♕e1 ♖f8 19.♕g3**

A pretty good advertisement for the theme 'Paralysing the Enemy Pieces'! **19...♘b4 20.♗xf5 exf5 21.e6+ ♖f6 22.♗xf6+ 1-0.**

Another great game that had obviously passed me by during my chess career was Ljubojevic's excellent win as White against Karpov at Turin 1982. The end of the game was particularly impressive, as you would have expected the colours to be reversed in this scenario!

Ljubomir Ljubojevic
Anatoly Karpov
Turin 1982

position after 31...♖ab8

A few moves earlier, Karpov had missed a (very necessary) chance for freedom, which involved going after the c4-pawn and allowing White to win the h7-pawn with ♘g5 and ♕xh7+. McDonald suggests that one of the differences between players of the 1980s and 2020s is that 'nowadays players are more willing to take liberties with the safety of their king to achieve positional aims.' I would also suggest that modern players very much follow the modern engine imperative of activity – even at the cost of material – above passivity. Ljubojevic now entrenches a rook in Black's position and probes Black general looseness in his dark squares. **32.♖db2 ♖xb2 33.♖xb2 f6 34.♖b6 ♕c7 35.♘h2**

A very nice move. The knight aims for g4 – attacking f6 – while freeing the f-pawn to defend e4 with f3. **35...♗c6 36.♘g4 ♖f8 37.f3 f5 38.exf5 ♖xf5 39.♕d2**

Restrained play from Ljubojevic. The queen returns to the fold, attacking d6 and threatening ♘h6+.

39...♔g7 40.♖xa6 e4 41.fxe4 ♖f7 42.e5 ♕c8 43.♕h6+

The queen returns and it will be fatal! **43...♔h8 44.e6 ♖g7 45.♖b6**

Black resigned. Super play!

An interesting book with a good range of examples. It's somewhere between 3 and 4 stars for me, but we'll stretch to 4!

■ ■ ■

'I will solve all the puzzles before I review it!' was my bold promise to myself, but I had to adjust my ambitions or face never writing about *Solving in*

Style by John Nunn (Gambit)! This is actually the second time I have read this book, though much to my shame all of the examples seemed completely unfamiliar to me! This is a substantially revised second edition, but I'm not sure that John has changed every single example so I have to conclude that my memory for puzzles is not as good as my memory for chess games!

I received the first edition as a gift from my friend Steve Giddins about 10 years ago, as a stimulus to get into problem solving competitions. I read it quite seriously but at some stage concluded that I didn't have the necessary puzzle solvers' hunger to really make a go of it. I think I'm a quite typical practical player in that I'm happy to solve a couple of problems, marvel at the ingenuity and then happily move on to some 'proper' chess!

However, this book remains the classic work to learn the technique of solving problems and studies. Nunn starts off with 2-movers, studies and 3-movers before really turning on the heat with longer problems and more complex studies. Subsequent chapters dive into the more exotic variants such as helpmates, selfmates and reflex-mates, series problems, retro-analytical problems and proof games. The book ends with a section on solving competi-

Solving in Style
New Expanded
Edition
John Nunn
Gambit, 2023
★★★★☆

tions and a last burst of puzzles for the reader to solve.

For me, problem solving still doesn't have the attraction that normal chess does but it has been a great pleasure

This book remains the classic work to learn the technique of solving problems and studies

working through a couple of examples a day, and reading Nunn's always clear explanations and hints about how to solve problems. There was one 2-move problem in particular that really stuck in my mind and I just have to share it with you!

White to play and win

I was quite slow to realise that Black is in zugzwang. If it were Black to move then the end would come swiftly: 1...d5 allows 2.♗d3 mate; 1...e6 allows 2.♘xd6 mate; 1...♔f5 allows 2.e4 mate. But how can White lose a move? 1.♖d1 allows 1...♔f5, 1.♕g8 allows 1...♔e3, 1.e3 allows 1...d5. Solving these problems really feels like trying to squash jelly! For me, it cost me 10 minutes before I finally cottoned on to the solution which you will find at the end of the article. I'm never going to forget this one!

An excellent book for anyone either looking to get seriously into problem solving, or for anyone (like me) just occasionally torturing their brain with a crazy-looking position! 4 solid stars. ∎

Solution:
1.♖a1!! introducing the threat of 2.♕b1 mate! Aaah, stunning!

Using the New In Chess app is easy!

- get early access to every issue
- replay all games in the Gameviewer

1

Sign in with your username and password to access the digital issue.

2

Read the articles, optimized for your screen size.

3

Select a move in the text to make the chess board appear. You can analyze the games with the built-in Stockfish engine.

The only chess magazine that moves
www.newinchess.com/chess-apps – for tablet, phone and PC

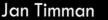
Jan Timman

A masterpiece by the brilliant Georgian study composer David Gurgenidze inspired Jan Timman to embark on a thematic journey. In all the studies that he presents there's a pawn that really should not be there.

The pawn that has to disappear

The Georgian grandmaster endgame composer David Gurgenidze will be 70 this year. He has authored a large number of magnificent endgame studies. At 21 years of age, he composed the following study.

David Gurgenidze
1st prize Shakhmaty (Riga) 1974

White to play and win

The starting move is obvious:
1.hxg7 Normally, starting a study with a capture is not considered *au fait*, but

in this case, there was little choice, since it's hardly possible to come up with a different starting move.

1...⬜g2+! Black's only chance. He must get rid of the h8-rook. To achieve this, the other rook must be sacrificed. Sacrificing the rook on h8 with check in order to prevent a pawn from queening is called the 'Prokes manoeuvre', after the Czech endgame composer Ladislav Prokes.

2.♔f1! The white king sets off on a long march. Insufficient was 2.♔xg2?, in view of 2...⬜xh2+! 3.♔xh2 ♗xf7 4.gxf7 ♔xf7 5.♘xd7 b3, and the black pawns are unstoppable, e.g. 6.♘e5+ ♔xg7 7.♘c4 (or 7.axb3 a3) 7...bxa2, and Black wins.
2...⬜f2+ 3.♔e1 ⬜e2+ 4.♔d1 ⬜d2+ 5.♔c1 ⬜c2+ 6.♔b1 ⬜b2+ 7.♔a1!

7...⬜xa2+ 8.♔b1 With the a-pawn gone, the white king returns.

8...⬜b2+ 9.♔c1 ⬜c2+ 10.♔d1 ⬜d2+ 11.♔e1 ⬜e2+ 12.♔f1 ⬜f2+ 13.♔g1 ⬜g2+

14.♔xg2! Only now!
14...⬜xh2+ 15.♔xh2 ♗xf7 16.gxf7 ♔xf7 17.♘xd7! b3 Or 17...a3 18.♘c5 a2 19.♘b3, and wins.
18.♘e5+! ♔xg7 19.♘c4!

Now everything becomes clear. With

the white a-pawn gone, White is able to block the black pawns. **19...b2 20.♘a3!** And wins.

In this study, Gurgenidze combines the Prokes manoeuvre with the theme of a disappearing pawn or piece, after which the same position arises again, but without that particular pawn or piece. In *Chess Curiosities*, Tim Krabbé describes this as follows: 'The way in which he allowed Black to execute his Prokes manoeuvre, that is, by getting rid of his pawn on a2, was itself a Prokes manoeuvre of sorts'.

The black rook that cannot be captured continually checking the enemy king from the second rank evokes an association: in the famous game Steinitz-Von Bardeleben, played in the legendary Hastings tournament of 1895, a white rook and the black king performed a similar dance on the seventh and eighth ranks, except from closer by.

For the sake of completeness I will give you the combination that started on move 21.

William Steinitz
Curt von Bardeleben
Hastings 1895

position after 20...g6

21.♘g5+ The start of the most famous combination in the history of chess. White forces the black king to return to e8.
21...♚e8 22.♖xe7+! This hammer blow seems to win at once, but Black still has a final resource.

Curt von Bardeleben (1861-1921) is mainly remembered for his spectacular loss to Steinitz at the Hastings tournament in 1895 (and the fact that he did not resign the game but simply walked out of the playing room never to return).

22...♚f8! Surprisingly enough, Black finds the only move to continue the fight. After 22...♚xe7 23.♖e1+ ♚d8 24.♘e6+ he would lose instantly.
23.♖f7+ ♚g8 24.♖g7+ ♚h8

25.♖xh7+ And here, Von Bardeleben stalked out of the playing hall. Black is hopelessly lost, e.g. 25...♚g8

The finish of Steinitz-Von Bardeleben inspired a study 123 years after the game

26.♖g7+ ♚f8 27.♘h7+, winning the queen.

Nowadays, there are some reservations about Steinitz's combination; the computer sees several alternative winning continuations that do little to stir the imagination. But it turned out to be useful as a starting-point for a study.

123 years after the famous game, Steffen Slumstrup Nielsen and Martin Minski composed the following study.

Steffen Slumstrup Nielsen & Martin Minski
1.p Bukovina-Rumania unification 100-AT 2018

White to play and win

Which king is more exposed? White's starting-move provides the answer.
1.♔d2 Preventing enemy checks, opening the c-file and attacking the black rook. Black has only one way to parry this.
1...♛f6 Covering the rook and threatening a devastating check on e2.
2.♖a1! White allows the check, something he can afford to do

because of his mating threat on a8. The alternative 2.♕c3+ wouldn't yield anything after 2...♔d8, and the black king has found safety.

2...♖e2+! Now it starts.

3.♔d1! ♖d2+

4.♔e1 The king sets off on a long march. We will see why later on.

4...♖e2+ 5.♔f1 ♖f2+ 6.♔g1 ♖xg2+ 7.♔f1 Now that Black has taken the pawn, the king returns – the same principle as in Gurgenidze's study!

7...♖f2+ 8.♔e1 ♖e2+ 9.♔d1 ♖d2+

10.♕xd2

White finally captures the rook.

10...♕xa1+ 11.♕c1+ ♕xc1+ 12.♔xc1 Now we see what the idea was all along: Black does not have the capture with ...hxg2.

12...♔d8 13.g7 And wins.

This study could be regarded as Von Bardeleben's revenge: this time the king moves do secure the win.

It seemed to me that this study had exhausted the theme of king march and rook checks. Three years ago, however, I came across a study in

Harold van der Heijden's database that gave me new insights.

Vladimir Klyukin
hm Zvyazda (Minsk) 1995

White to play and win

Materially, things are equal. White's starting-move is obvious: he must control the long diagonal.

1.♕f3 ♕xa7 Forced. **2.♖d7** It seems as if White has an easy win.

2...♕b7! Checking the white king was pointless, since 2...♕a1+ would simply be met by 3.♖d1. The text is a great resource, but White has a suitable answer.

3.♖h7+! This, too, is Steinitz-Von Bardeleben!

The brilliant Georgian grandmaster endgame composer David Gurgenidze hopes to celebrate his 70th birthday this year.

3...♕xh7 4.♕c3+ ♔g8 5.♘f6+ ♔h8 6.♘xh7+ And wins.

I felt that the fantastic ...♕a7-b7! deserved a better fate. In other words: it should be possible to compose a winning study with that move. This led me back to Nielsen and Minski's study; it should be possible to allow the queen sacrifice to win, while at the same time making the pawn disappear based on a different motif. This resulted in the following study.

Jan Timman
sp. p. UAPA 2021

White to play and win

A sharp position. **1.h6** A pawn advance to corner the black king.

1...♕d8 The only defence. Black must counter the threats on the back rank and the long diagonal.

2.♖a1! A deeply thought-out move.

I felt that the fantastic ... ♛a7-b7! deserved a better fate. It should be possible to compose a winning study with that move

After 2.♕a1+ f6 3.♖d1 ♔g8 4.h3 ♖e4 5.♔xg2 ♕d5 Black wouldn't be too bad.

2...♕f6+ The alternative 2...♘xe3 is insufficient in view of 3.♕b2+ ♖d4 4.♗xe3 ♕h4+ 5.♔f1 ♕h3+ 6.♔g2 ♕xg2+ 7.♔xg2 ♖d8 8.♖a6!, and White wins the endgame. The h6-pawn loses nothing of its strength in the endgame.

3.♔e2 ♘f4+! This knight sacrifice gives the black rook access to the second rank.

4.exf4 ♖g2+ 5.♔f1 ♖xd2 It looks as if Black has solved all his problems, but now it's time for Klyukin's move.

6.♕b2!! Pinning the black queen and opening the a-file for the rook.
6...♖f2+ 7.♔g1 ♖g2+ 8.♔h1 ♖xh2+ 9.♔g1 The now familiar motif.

9...♖g2+ 10.♕xg2 ♕xa1+ 11.♔h2 Now it is revealed why the h-pawn had to disappear: the h2-square has been made available to the king. It's a remarkable situation; Black is four pawns up and there are no concrete mating threats, and yet there is no way for him to prevent the eventual mate.
11...♔g8 12.♕d5! Devastating centralization. One simple line is 12...♕b2+ 13.♔g3 ♕c3+ 14.♔g4 ♔f8 15.♕d8 mate.

I wasn't fully satisfied, though. The study lacked economy, and the foreplay diverted attention from the main theme. When Judit Polgar organized a tournament for game-based studies last year, I grabbed my chance and composed a study based on the same theme but with a better structure.

Jan Timman
Global Chess Festival 2022

White to play and win

A clear position; the starting-move is obvious.
1.a6 ♕c6 The only way to parry the white threats.
1...♕c8 would be met by the devastating 2.♕d6.
2.♕g2!! This is familiar – the start of the dance of rook and king.
2...♖xe2+ 3.♔d1 ♖d2+

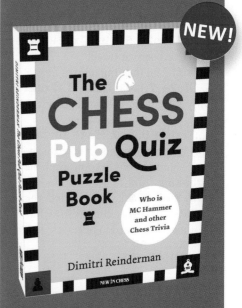

4.♔c1 ♖c2+ 5.♔b1 ♖xb2+ The pawn has been captured.
6.♔c1! And the king returns.
6...♖c2+ 7.♔d1 ♖d2+ 8.♕xd2! Only now does White capture the rook.
8...♕xh1+ 9.♔c2 ♕e4+ 10.♔b2 This is why the b-pion had to disappear: square b2 has become available to the king.
10...♕e7 Black has parried the threats for now, but White has another trump card to play.

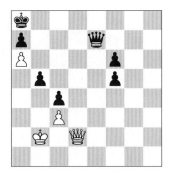

11.♕h2! A switchback, as the jargon has it. The queen returns to its original square. This move takes away square b8 from the black king

and threatens mate on h8. **11...♕g7** The only defence. **12.♕d6** The death blow. **12...♕g2+ 13.♔a3** And wins.

ChessBase India showed this study to a number of top players, who successfully identified the secret of the pawn that had to disappear. I was pleased to learn that they were appreciative of my study.

A few months after Judit's festival, I found an old study by Gurgenidze in which he shows how a pawn needs to disappear in order to make room for another piece: the queen.

David Gurgenidze
1. sp. p. Golden Fleece 1986

White to play and win

This is my version of the study, in which I have left out the white pawn on h6 and moved the king from g8 to h8.
1.c7 Of course. Now Black must try to at least stop a pawn.
1...♖e3+ 2.♔f1! The start of the king march. After 2.♔d1 ♖xd3+ 3.♔c1 ♖db3 4.c8♕+ ♔h7 5.♕xd7+ ♔h6 White would be unable to win.
2...♖f3+ 3.♔g1 ♖g3+ 4.♔h1 ♖xh3+

5.♔g1 Only now does the white king move towards the queenside.

5...♖g3+ 6.♔f1 ♖f3+ 7.♔e1 ♖e3+ 8.♔d1 ♖xd3+ 9.♔c1 ♖db3 10.c8♕+ ♔h7 11.♕xd7+ ♔h6

12.♕h3+!
And this was the idea. The h-pawn had to disappear to make this check possible.
12...♔g7 13.♕c3+! The theme repeats itself.
13...♔h7 14.♕xb2 And wins.

The black rook operated on the third rank here, but this is not a fundamental difference. ∎

SOLUTIONS of page 79 The Worst Move on the Board

1. Humphries-Blower, Wolverhampton and District League, 2015. **66.c8♕!!** with stalemate.
2. Bruzon-Vidit, FIDE World Cup, Baku 2015. **38...♘f4!!** allowing 39.♘g4 mate.
3. Vidit-Bruzon, FIDE World Cup, Baku 2015. **57.♗d5!!** allowing 57...♕c7+ 0-1 (58.♕d6 ♕xd6 mate).
4. Spitzl-Isserman, Bad Homburg 2015. **62...♔d5!!** allowing 63.c4+ 1-0

(63...♔d4 64.♕e3 mate).
5. Jimenez-Teichmann, Sant Martí 2016. **23...g6!!** allowing 24.♕xh7+ 1-0 (24...♔xh7 25.♖h4+ ♔g8 26.♖h8 mate).
6. Internet game, 2020, game score unavailable. **1.♖g4!!** allowing several wins, e.g. 1...f5, 1...♖xg4+ and 2...f5(+), 1...♔f5 or 1...♔h5 2.h4 ♖g6.
7. García-Ivkov, Capablanca Memorial,

Havana, 1965. **36...d3!!** allowing 37.♗c3 1-0 (37...♘d4 38.♗xd4 ♕xf1+ 39.♔xf1 and 40.♕g7 mate).
8. Tarling-Quinn, 4NCL online, 2021. **38...b6!!** allowing 39.b5 (which was not played) and White promotes.
9. Hassomal Daswani-Crocker, Gibraltar 2019. **31...♖g5!!** allowing 32.♕e8+ ♔h7 33.♘xg5+ hxg5 34.hxg5+ 1-0 (34...♖h3 35.♖xh3 mate).

They are The Champions

BOKANG MOTSAMAI
Lesotho

No one can say that life has been perfect for Bokang Motsamai. He lost his father at an early age, and he's long been hobbled by financial issues. But the 17-year-old from Lesotho, a small landlocked country in sub-Saharan Africa, won't let hardships prevent him from achieving his chess goals, and the first-place victory he scored at the Lesotho National Championships in April is proof of that.

'In life, there are problems to overcome, and chess players, especially, should have faith in overcoming them', Bokang said.

High up on the list of difficulties for Bokang, really, has been money. When he was two years old, his father died of a brain tumour because his family couldn't pay for proper treatment. In addition, Bokang has had to leave school several times because he couldn't afford tuition. He also couldn't pay for a chess coach for the recent Lesotho championships. However, not being able to afford a coach only spurred him to study his chess harder.

And the hard work paid off.

Even though Bokang was the fourth-seeded player going into the tournament, which was held between April 14th and 16th in Maseru, Lesotho's capital, he scored an impressive six points of seven and beat out the top seed.

As far as the future goes, Bokang wants to become a master and perhaps one day play under the Russian or Spanish flag. He's currently learning Russian and Spanish and hopes to be fluent in them in three years.

Be that as it may, Bokang still faces some challenges. A one-year scholastic scholarship he received in 2021 (thanks to his chess achievements) wasn't enough to cover all of his tuition debts (about 500 euros), and his diploma won't be released to him until the debts are paid. Bokang hopes to go to university to study computer science.

Until then, though, he says he will use the mental fortitude chess has taught him to try and overcome obstacles. 'Through chess, I've learned to believe in my choices, and I will continue to trust myself.'

In the championship, Bokang defeated top seed Sechaba Khalema with a sequence of powerful pawn pushes.

In **They are The Champions** we pay tribute to national champions across the globe. For suggestions please write to editors@newinchess.com.

Bokang Motsamai (1569)
Khalema Sechaba (1765)
Lesotho 2023

position after 24....♘b8

25.c5!
A forceful breakthrough thanks to the indirect protection of the pawn on d5.
25...bxc5 26.bxc5 dxc5 27.♖xc5 ♔g7 28.♖b3 ♖f7 29.d6
The pawn remains untouchable.
29...♘d7 30.♖c7 ♘f8 31.♖bb7 ♖xc7 32.dxc7 ♖c8 33.♗b3 a5 34.a4 h6 35.h3 g5 36.g4 fxg4 37.hxg4

Black is completely in zugzwang. Any move he will make loses, so he resigned. ∎

Vladimir Fedoseev

CURRENT ELO: 2676

DATE OF BIRTH: February 16, 1995

PLACE OF BIRTH: St. Petersburg

PLACE OF RESIDENCE: Spain

What is your favourite city?
I don't have a favourite city yet, but the most impressive one was certainly Rome.

What was the last great meal you had?
I like different kinds of food, so it would be strange to me to choose a favourite.

What drink brings a smile to your face?
It only takes a few drinks to make me sad. Normally I am smiling quite often.

Which book would you give to a friend?
Something motivational like *The Mamba Mentality* by Kobe Bryant or *The No Asshole Rule* by Robert Sutton.

What book are you currently reading?
I am quite lazy to read books, but I read poetry online or search for good articles.

What is your all-time favourite movie?
Without any doubt *Star Wars*, the old ones, episodes 1-6.

And your favourite TV series?
The last one I liked a lot was the mini-series *The Loudest Voice*.

Do you have a favourite actor?
Someone from the old guard, Sylvester Stallone or Al Pacino.

And a favourite actress?
My wife is the best actress in my life, always surprising and great to watch.

What music do you listen to?
From rap and R&B to classical music, depending on my mood.

Is there a work of art that moves you?
I am more a fan of mind games and writing than works of art.

What is your earliest chess memory?
My first lesson in the chess club Brig in Petergof more than 20 years ago.

Who is your favourite chess player?
It's hard to understand everything that was played by others, but as a role model – maybe Viktor Korchnoi.

Is there a chess book that had a profound influence on you?
Dva Matcha (Two Matches) by Kasparov, my first book (by Botvinnik) and Bronstein's book on Zurich 1953.

What was your best result ever?
Hopefully that result does not exist yet.

What was the most exciting chess game you ever saw?
Chess is always exciting if you look for nuances.

What is your favourite square?
Any, depending on the game ☺.

What are chess players particularly good at (except for chess)?
All mind games, analytical work and maybe investments.

Do you have any superstitions?
Sometimes I can feel if it will be a good day for me or not.

Facebook, Instagram, Snapchat, or?
Facebook and memes on Instagram.

How many friends do you have on Facebook?
More than 2000.

Who do you follow on Twitter?
Nobody, since I am not on Twitter.

What is your life motto?
Trust the process☺.

When were you happiest?
When I won my first Russian Rapid Championship U-12, I felt confident that my chess career was going to be great from then on.

When was the last time you cried?
During the first days after the invasion, realizing there is a lot pain and death every day.

Who or what would you like to be if you weren't yourself?
A yogi, because it's a great way to live, in my opinion.

Is there something you'd love to learn?
Baduk, poker (Omaha or Texas), history, new cultures.

What would people be surprised to know about you?
I was considered to be an invalid after I was born.

What is your favourite place in the world?
Spain, the Costa Blanca, Valencia, everywhere around here.

What is your greatest fear?
That humans will destroy themselves.

And your greatest regret?
Being lazy, but it's still my usual behaviour ☺

What is the best thing that was ever said about chess?
Hopefully in 30 years from now I will be able to answer this question. I am still learning the game.